DIARY OF A MISFIT PENGUIN

DIARY OF A MISFIT PENGUIN

WENDY GARDNER

DIARY OF A MISFIT PENGUIN

ISBN 979-8-218-88161-0

CONTENTS

INTRODUCTION

AUTHOR'S NOTE

I still remember the first time I stepped onto the platform at Euston Station. I was a young Glaswegian lassie with dreams that felt far too big for my cheap suitcase, stepping off the train into a swirl of city sounds that felt absolutely electrifying. Back then, I believed that if I worked hard enough and said "yes" to every single opportunity, success would arrive quickly. I didn't realise that I was stepping into a role that would eventually cost me my own sense of self.

For years, I lived in "machine mode," a state of being where I was relentlessly driven, indispensable, and utterly unstoppable. I wore "busy" like a suit of protective armour and took being called "the machine" as a twisted badge of honour. I thought strength meant burying pain and that emotions were a liability I simply couldn't afford.

But machines can’t love, and eventually, they break.

My unravelling didn't happen all at once. It came in the "shattering moments" of real life. It was the silence in a delivery room when my daughter, Hannah, was born sleeping. It was a motorway crash on an ordinary Tuesday that finally forced me to admit, "Actually, I’m not okay."

And it was the day my own daughter looked in the mirror and whispered, "Mum, I don’t feel beautiful," using a voice of self-doubt she had learned by watching me.

I wrote this book because I spent too long trying to solve the wrong puzzle. I tried to outrun my own sorrow with speed, only to find that grief always waits you out.

In the pages that follow, I want to share my mission for human sustainability that has become my life's work. We are living in an era of "greedy jobs" that demand our undivided loyalty and constant availability. We treat the planet's resources with more care than we treat our own bodies and minds. This book is my toolkit for anyone who feels like a flamingo trapped in a penguin suit... bright, vibrant, and "too much" for a world that demands conformity.

You will find research here, but more importantly, you will find small, daily rituals and the simple acts to reset your nervous system. These are the practices that helped me tremendously.

Today, through my work at The Ohana Foundation, I help women and girls discover who they are and learn to love themselves courageously. We help stuck adults get unstuck. I no longer work with machines. I work with humans.

If you are reading this, perhaps you are also waiting for permission to apply for your own life. This is it. You don't need to be unstoppable. You just need to be human again.

Wendy Gardner

CHAPTER 1

FROM HUMAN TO MACHINE

THE MACHINE TAKES OVER

"If the world is to be healed through human efforts, I am convinced it will be by ordinary people, people whose love for this life is even greater than their fear." — Joanna Macy, environmental activist and author

I can still picture that moment when I first stepped onto the platform at Euston Station. A young Glaswegian lassie with massive dreams, stepping off the train into this incredible swirl of city sounds. Taxis honking everywhere, tourists dragging their luggage behind them, and this general bustle that was absolutely electrifying. My heart was hammering against my ribcage, caught somewhere between raw excitement and nerves so tight they felt ready to snap.

Growing up in Glasgow had its wonders. I was surrounded by this brilliant, close-knit community, constant laughter, and my dad's larger-than-life presence filling every room. But he was also protective to the point where it felt controlling. He wanted me close to home, safe in all the routines he'd carefully set up for me. Moving to London was definitely not part of his plan. Yet I was equally determined that it absolutely would be part of mine.

I think we all reach those moments when we realise we've got a choice. Either stay put in my comfort zone, or leap towards something bigger. For me, that leap was a train ticket south.

Those first few weeks in London were exhilarating. Everything seemed so much bigger. The roads, the buildings, this incredible global swirl of different accents I'd hear on every single corner. I'd managed to find an entry-level job at a retailer's head office, just an assistant role really, mostly spreadsheets and phone calls. But I felt like I'd absolutely made it.

I was completely convinced that if I worked hard enough and said yes to every single opportunity that came my way, success would arrive quickly.

Early on, I got this reputation for being that bold, relentlessly driven Scottish girl. I'd volunteer for the late shifts, extra projects, absolutely anything going. My thinking was pretty simple really. If you want something, you show them you're completely indispensable.

My colleagues would tease me sometimes. "Wendy, do you ever actually sleep?" But there was this sparkle in their eyes when they said it. They admired the tenacity, even if it was probably a bit naive.

I'd hear managers saying things like "We want to breed our own talent," and my head would snap up immediately. Breed me then! I'm right here!

I remember marching into HR one day and announcing "I want to be a buyer." I was absolutely trembling inside because I was still so junior, but I masked it with complete bravado. To my surprise, they actually took me seriously enough to schedule psychometric tests and proper interviews. I passed every single one. That moment was my first real taste of how my courage could actually open doors.

As an assistant buyer, I was completely on fire. I travelled constantly for the job, negotiating deals with suppliers all over the place, curating these amazing product ranges to bring back to UK stores. I was loving every single late night. I felt absolutely unstoppable.

Looking back now, though, there was this clear undercurrent running through everything. I was so hungry for success that I'd override any sign of exhaustion or stress.

Those late-night calls back home to Glasgow would often end with me brushing off my dad's concerns. "No, I'm absolutely fine, just busy!" Busy became like this protective armour I wore.

Eventually, after I'd proved myself at Dixons over seven years and been promoted to Senior Buyer, I got tempted away by this American retailer when it became clear there was no path to Director. It was a complete whirlwind. Absolutely frenetic in every sense. But after ten months I'd had enough. When I left there, Tesco came calling.

At the time, Tesco was huge in groceries but not yet the global juggernaut we know today. They needed someone to help expand their non-food categories in the UK and internationally, and my experience seemed to fit perfectly. That's when I discovered I was four months pregnant.

For weeks, I'd been feeling really off. Fatigued...nauseous...I chalked it up to the stress of Christmas festivities. Then the GP told me quite plainly "You're nearly halfway through a pregnancy."

My first thought was complete panic. This doesn't fit my plan at all. My career is supposed to be my baby. But life doesn't always follow the script we've carefully crafted in our heads, does it? I rang the headhunter to cancel the Tesco interview, explaining "I'm four months pregnant." She told me to hold on and let her speak to them. To my absolute amazement, Tesco still wanted me. I went to the interview with my tiny bump showing and was completely stunned when they offered me the job on the spot, even planning a travel schedule around my due date.

Looking back, that was probably the first sign I was stepping into an environment that would completely challenge my illusions of control. Maybe I should have slowed down properly. Truly paused to savour the absolute preciousness of carrying a child.

But I was so locked into what I now call "Machine Mode." I was so utterly convinced that stopping would completely erode my shot at success. I pushed that pregnancy into the corner of my mind. I carried on with the Tesco induction and forged ahead as though I weren't pregnant at all.

I was 38 weeks along when this crushing sense of dread descended. Hannah, my unborn daughter, was unusually active the night before, rolling and kicking in ways that felt almost frantic. My back ached with this pain I can't fully describe. Some part of me just knew something was terribly wrong. I went to the hospital expecting mild reassurance from the midwife.

I can still see the sonographer's face as she scanned my belly. Her expression shifted completely. Concern etched in every line around her eyes. There were these quiet murmurings between nurses and a heavy feeling in the air. Then the words just tumbled out. "I'm so sorry. There's no heartbeat. We need to induce labour."

I felt this wave of confusion. I was in complete disbelief. Then this hollow ache where my heart used to be. No heartbeat? How could Hannah possibly be gone? I was preparing for her birth and all the chaos of new motherhood. Not arranging a funeral for a stillborn child.

The labour that followed was brutal in every possible way. I remember hearing my own wails echoing through the delivery room. The raw painfelt completely inhuman. I had never known heartbreak like that before. For days afterwards, I moved around in this complete fog. All the illusions I'd been clinging to, that I could outrun vulnerability, that I had everything under perfect control, were just shattered. My body had failed at what should be the most natural job imaginable. At least, that's how I made sense of it at the time.

Tesco, to their credit, gave me a three-month leave of absence. But it felt completely surreal. I barely knew my colleagues really. Most of them were just polite strangers. My boss would ring occasionally and gently ask "How are you coping?" I had absolutely no words. I'd lost Hannah, and with her, I'd lost some fundamental sense of who I actually was.

At the end of those three months, my boss, who was under enormous pressure herself, told me "Wendy, we really need you back. We're sending you to the Czech Republic next week for a product sourcing trip." I murmured "I can't," but she was completely insistent. "You can." My mind was spinning. At the same time, I desperately wanted to run from my grief. Work beckoned like this perfect distraction.

I said yes.

THE UNRAVELLING

I boarded that plane with heartbreak coiled so tightly inside me. I buried Hannah's memory as deep as I possibly could. From the outside, it probably looked like incredible resilience. "Wow, Wendy's absolutely unstoppable!" But from the inside, it was emotional suppression of the highest order. I poured myself completely into this role of "corporate machine." I solved every crisis. I led every expansion. I measured myself in results. I delivered them daily. If I stayed busy enough, I could stave off the anguish that was threatening to completely engulf me. Or so I thought.

People at Tesco started calling me "the machine." Half jokingly, half in genuine awe. I took it as this twisted badge of honour. I had absolutely no space to cry or process anything. I was either in a meeting, on a flight, or glued to my laptop at midnight. This is what success requires, I kept telling myself. Emotions felt like a massive liability I simply couldn't afford.

Underneath, though, I was fracturing. Grief doesn't vanish because we want it to. It festers and grows. In those private moments, alone in foreign hotel rooms, I'd sometimes just crumble, tears softly erupting like hot lava from a dormant volcano. But come morning, the mask was back in place. Suit pressed, hair combed. My unstoppable persona was fully engaged.

Over time, I learned to compartmentalise absolutely everything. I was "corporate Wendy," this machine at work. Years later, after I later gave birth to my second daughter, I was "mum Wendy," doing my absolute best to be nurturing despite this fear lodged deep inside that something else might go catastrophically wrong. But I never integrated these parts of myself. That's the real hallmark of "machine mode." You split yourself into these separate segments. Each one designed to handle a specific domain. Never allowing them to actually overlap.

If I'd had proper guidance, or quite frankly, if I'd allowed myself to actually accept it, I might have sought grief counselling or taken a break from the relentless pace. But I was too angry and scared. Actually, I was completely numb. One attempt to schedule NHS counselling ended with this long waiting list. I walked away muttering "Fine, I'll handle it on my own." Except "handling it" really meant ignoring it completely.

I'm sharing this story because it highlights how someone can appear completely high-functioning, even admired for their resilience, whilst carrying this immense hidden pain. Society often labels that kind of behaviour as "strength." Yet it's also this refusal to feel. In fact, it's mostly an attempt to become something inhuman.

Grief will not be outrun forever though. It seeps into our bones, surfaces in mysterious ways, and creeps into our dreams at night. My facade cracked slowly over the years, manifesting in chronic health issues and these bouts of intense anxiety I couldn't logically explain. Only with proper distance can I see that burying my grief actually stunted me. It stole away joy and connection in the process.

What Hannah's short life and devastating loss ultimately taught me is that I was not truly in control. None of us are. We can plan all we like, but reality can still completely blindside us. The key isn't to respond by further tightening the reins, as I did, but by learning to meet our vulnerability with proper compassion. Because being human means being vulnerable. That's where true empathy, resilience, and growth reside.

So if you find yourself in that same trap, constantly "on," burying heartache behind your achievements, know two things. First, you're absolutely not alone. Second, it's completely unsustainable. Eventually, you have to face whatever you're running from. By opening that emotional door, you might discover this deeper well of strength and humanity you never knew existed.

This chapter is called "From Machine to Human" because losing Hannah was the moment life forced me to confront that in trying to be unstoppable, I lost a piece of my soul.

THE HIDDEN SIGNS

You know that feeling when you get home from work and realise you can't remember the drive? Or when someone asks what you did today and you struggle to recall anything beyond a blur of meetings and emails? That's machine mode in action. We think we're being productive, but we're actually running on autopilot, disconnected from ourselves and everything around us.

The ability to push through endless days without feeling much of anything used to be my superpower. I didn't understand that machine mode was making my stress worse. It created a cycle that slowly eroded my mental health without me even realising it.

Researchers have been studying this phenomenon for years, though they use different language to describe it. They talk about psychological detachment and emotional exhaustion, but they're examining what happens when we get stuck in survival mode and can't find our way back to being human. A 2023 study of over 700 teachers revealed something interesting about how this disconnection affects our mental health and what we can do about it.

The study found that people who couldn't mentally switch off from work during their personal time were more likely to experience emotional exhaustion, which then led to depressive symptoms. Their conclusion was that our inability to truly disconnect from work creates a specific kind of emotional depletion that changes our brain chemistry.

The teachers in this study were experiencing what the researchers called emotional exhaustion, which is far more serious than ordinary tiredness. It's a chronic state where your emotional resources become completely depleted. You stop feeling joy, excitement, or even sadness. Everything becomes muted and grey. You're functioning, but you're not really living.

In this case, psychological detachment acted as a form of protection. Teachers who could genuinely switch off from work thoughts during their personal time had lower levels of emotional exhaustion and fewer depressive symptoms. In other words, it's not enough to just physically leave work. You have to mentally disconnect too.

Machine mode tricks us into thinking we're being responsible by staying mentally connected to work all day and night. We check emails during dinner and think through tomorrow's presentations whilst trying to fall asleep. We tell ourselves this makes us more prepared, but the research shows it's destroying our ability to recover.

The study revealed the role of self compassion in breaking this cycle. Teachers who were kind to themselves when facing difficulties showed remarkable resilience against the effects of emotional exhaustion. When they did experience work related stress, those with higher self compassion were far less likely to develop depressive symptoms.

The teachers with high self compassion didn't judge themselves or push harder. They acknowledged their struggle as a normal human response to stress. They treated themselves with care. This simple shift created a buffer against burnout and depression.

Machine mode makes us lose the ability to be present with our own experience. We stop noticing when we're tired, stressed, or overwhelmed. We disconnect from our bodies and emotions. The research shows this disconnection has real consequences for our mental health, but it also points toward surprisingly simple solutions.

RECLAIMING YOUR HUMANITY

We've all been there. You're at work, putting on a brave face. Inside you're crumbling. A difficult customer is shouting at you. You smile and nod. Your colleague is having a meltdown. Suddenly you're the one trying to calm them down whilst managing your own stress. This is what happens when we shift into "machine mode." We become emotional robots, constantly managing our feelings and others' feelings too. It's exhausting, and frankly, it's making people sick.

I used to think this was just part of being professional. Keep your emotions in check. Help others with theirs. Push through the day. But after years of watching people burn out around me, I started wondering if there was a better way.

Think about your typical workday. How much time do you spend managing emotions? Not just your own, but your colleagues', your customers', maybe even your boss's? If you work in any job where you interact with people, you're doing what researchers call "emotion regulation." It sounds fancy, but it's actually something we all do constantly without realising it.

There are two main types of emotion regulation. First, there's managing your own emotions. This might mean reframing a stressful situation to feel better about it, or suppressing your real feelings to appear professional. Then there's managing other people's emotions. This could involve helping a colleague see a situation differently, or controlling how others express their emotions around you.

Researchers studied this phenomenon with aged care workers in Australia. These people faced some of the most emotionally demanding situations imaginable. They were dealing with clients who were physically deteriorating. Family members of these clients were stressed. Sometimes they would take it out on staff. It was emotional management on steroids.

The study looked at 336 aged care employees and found that when these workers had to manage other people's emotions, gratitude acted like a protective shield against burnout. When they were dealing with other people's emotional chaos, gratitude helped in several ways.

Grateful people experienced more positive emotions throughout their day. These positive feelings acted like a buffer against the drain of managing difficult people. It was like having an emotional bank account with extra funds to draw from. Gratitude also made the care workers more likely to help others.

Grateful people are better at reframing difficult situations. Instead of seeing an aggressive client as a personal attack, you might see them as someone who's scared or in pain. This shift in perspective makes the emotional labour less draining. Perhaps most importantly, positive emotions from gratitude can actually "undo" the stress response from negative interactions. It's like having a reset button for your emotional system.

Some people naturally become the person others turn to for emotional support. If that's you, gratitude could help prevent you from burning out whilst still being able to help your colleagues. If you're managing a team, understanding that emotional labour is real work that depletes people can help you better support your team. Recognising and appreciating the emotional work your employees do, and helping them develop gratitude practices, could improve both wellbeing and performance.

This research points to something important about modern work. We've created jobs that require enormous amounts of emotional labour, but we rarely acknowledge or support this aspect of work. We train people in technical skills but ignore the emotional skills they need to thrive, not just survive. The aged care workers in this study dealt with some of the most emotionally challenging work imaginable. Yet the research showed that simple practices like gratitude could make a real difference in whether they burnt out or flourished.

So what can you actually do with this information? Simply noticing and appreciating small positive moments throughout your workday can begin to build those emotional reserves. When you're dealing with difficult people, try to find something to appreciate about the interaction.

Sometimes, when you're stuck in that machine mode, finding genuine gratitude feels impossible. Your nervous system is so wound up from managing everyone else's emotions that you can barely think straight. That's where something I discovered called Emotional Freedom Technique (EFT), or tapping, becomes incredibly powerful. It's one of the most effective ways I've found to access gratitude, especially when everything feels overwhelming.

Most of us try to fix ourselves from the top down. We say positive things to ourselves when we're anxious. We picture success whilst our stomach is in knots. It's still tense. It's still waiting for something bad to happen. But you can't think your way out when your body is stuck in defence mode. Your nervous system controls real change. That's why EFT works so well. It talks directly to your nervous system.

Pick something specific that's bothering you right now. Maybe you're frustrated with your boss, or doubting whether you're good enough at your job. Give that feeling a number from zero to ten based on how intense it feels.

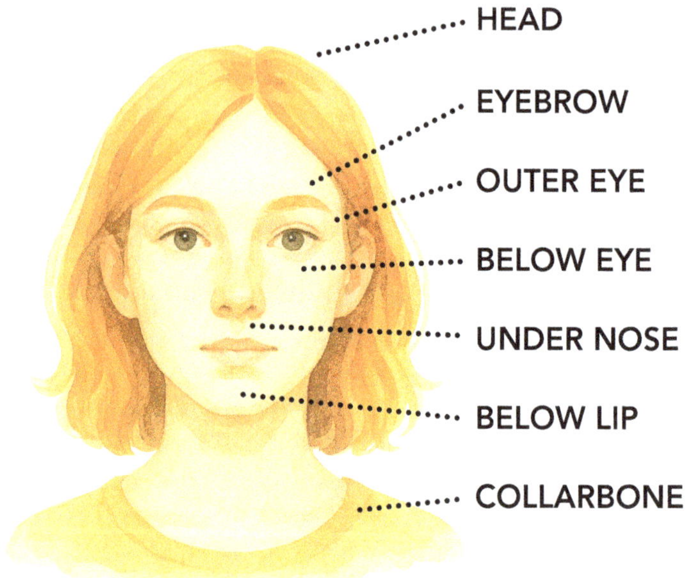

Now use your fingertips to tap gently on the edge of your hand below your pinky finger on your karate chop point. Whilst you're tapping, say something like "Even though I feel this knot in my stomach about tomorrow's meeting, I choose to accept and respect myself."

Then move to other spots on your face and body. The start of your eyebrow point near your nose. The side of your eye. Under your eye on your bone. Between your nose and upper lip. Under your lower lip. Your collarbone. Under your arm, just below your armpit.

Keep tapping and keep talking about whatever comes up. Notice what you're feeling. After a few rounds of acknowledging the difficult emotions, you can start tapping and focusing on what you appreciate. "Even though work has been stressful, I'm grateful for this colleague who always has my back." "Even though that customer was difficult, I appreciate that I handled it with kindness."

This combination of gentle touch and honest emotional expression essentially tells your body it's safe to stop panicking and start noticing good things again. When you acknowledge what you're feeling first, you interrupt the stress spiral that keeps you trapped in survival mode. Your body gets the message that the emergency is over, and suddenly there's space for genuine gratitude to emerge.

THE CRASH

The car crash happened on an ordinary morning rush, the kind where nothing feels particularly significant until everything changes. Rush hour traffic had ground to its familiar halt ahead of me, brake lights bleeding red through the rising sun. I pressed my brake pedal, but the driver behind me didn't react quickly enough. The impact jolted my neck and sent adrenaline surging through my system like electricity through water, making my hands shake uncontrollably as I pulled over to the hard shoulder.

We exchanged details in that peculiar dance of post accident politeness, both rattled but mercifully uninjured. The damage to my car required repairs but left it drivable. I had a complete mental breakdown. My entire life hinged on this daily commute. One mishap could collapse everything I'd built. If I couldn't drive, how would I reach work? If I couldn't work, how would I support my daughter? The questions circled like vultures.

The next day, I woke with a stiff neck and unexpected resolve burning in my chest. I arrived late to the office, eyes stinging with suppressed tears that threatened to spill at any moment.

When my boss asked with genuine concern about whether I was all right, the usual response lodged in my throat like a stone. Instead of the automatic reassurance, I croaked out the truth. "Actually, I'm not."

That small admission felt terrifying. I'd just stepped off a cliff into thin air. Would they perceive me as weak? Unreliable? But it also felt liberating, like throwing open windows in a suffocating room and letting fresh air flood in. The crash became my turning point. It was the moment my facade finally cracked wide enough to let light through.

I contacted a therapist, something I'd attempted briefly after losing Hannah but abandoned in frustration when healing didn't arrive on schedule. This time, I committed to the messy, nonlinear process of genuine recovery. I showed up week after week, even when progress felt invisible.

In those sessions, surrounded by tissues, I realised how thoroughly I'd normalised living on the precipice of collapse. Psychologically, I existed in a state of hypervigilance. The therapist helped me understand that I was exhausted from wearing a mask. I'd been running on fumes for so long that I'd forgotten what actual fuel felt like.

HUMAN CONNECTION

I used to think exhaustion was simply about working too many hours. Take a holiday, have a lie-in, switch off your phone for the weekend. That's what everyone prescribed, wasn't it? But something always felt off about this advice. I'd take the time off, lie on a beach somewhere lovely, and still feel completely drained. The exhaustion went deeper than hours logged at the office.

Then I came across Brené Brown's work with leaders inside the US military, and one story in particular completely shifted my understanding. Air Force Colonel DeDe Halfhill noticed her squadron kept telling her they were "tired." The obvious solution would've been more rest and recuperation. Send them home early. Give them extra leave. But after reading research about how workplace exhaustion often masks loneliness, she asked a different question entirely. "Who here feels lonely?" Hands went up across the room.

That single question changed everything. What looked like fatigue was actually isolation. If she'd sent those airmen home alone for more rest, she might've amplified the very thing that was hurting them. They didn't need more hours off. They needed connection. Brown's larger point is around the language of leadership. When we choose human words (lonely, connected, belonging) people feel seen, and the real problems surface. When we hide behind sterile corporate speak (tempo, throughput, productivity) we miss what's actually going on beneath the surface. That shift in language opened a completely different conversation in DeDe's unit. They could build connection on purpose.

I thought about my own experience through this lens. All those years at Tesco, people calling me "the machine," working myself into the ground. How many times did I describe myself as "tired" or "busy" when what I really meant was "I feel completely alone with this pressure"? How often did I prescribe myself more time off that I never truly took, or if I did take it, spent it anxiously checking emails anyway?

Brown also uncovered something fascinating about how military leadership language had evolved over decades. A 1948 Air Force leadership manual talked plainly about belonging, compassion, kindness, even love. By the time modern doctrine came around, those words had been completely bled out. We didn't stop feeling these things. We just pretended feelings weren't part of professional life anymore. And we paid for it with disengagement, isolation, and this quiet despair that nobody wanted to name.

This sanitisation of language is not unique to the military. It had infected corporate culture too. We'd replaced "I'm struggling" with "bandwidth issues." We'd swapped "I need help" for "resource allocation challenges." We'd turned ourselves into walking corporate dictionaries, and in doing so, we'd lost the ability to actually connect with each other as humans.

Since discovering this research, Brown's ideas have been implemented across military units. Army Resiliency Day forums were built around her work. Leadership training where officers are explicitly taught to "rumble" with vulnerability, build trust, and name emotions accurately.

Why does this matter for those of us trapped in machine mode? Because I lived the flip side of this equation for years. I kept prescribing myself more output, efficiency, and "time off" that I never genuinely used. I thought if I could just optimise my schedule better, or find the perfect work-life balance formula, the exhaustion would lift. But what I actually needed was the courage to say "I'm not okay" and let people in.

Machine mode tells us to recharge alone and come back tougher. Brown's research, and DeDe's experience, suggests another route entirely. Get honest, get specific, and get connected. That's where recovery actually starts.

RE-LEARNING TO BE HUMAN

When I first arrived in London as a young woman from Glasgow, I believed that success meant becoming unstoppable. I thought strength was about pushing through pain and that the best way to handle difficult emotions was to simply work harder. I was wrong about all of it.

The research I've shared throughout this chapter validates what took me years to understand through painful experience. The studies on emotional exhaustion show that our inability to mentally disconnect from work creates measurable changes in our brain chemistry. When we stay psychologically tethered to our jobs during personal time, we systematically deplete our emotional resources until we're running on empty. The university teachers who maintained their mental health learnt that genuine recovery requires self compassion.

My own journey from ambitious assistant to "the machine" illustrates how easy it is to mistake emotional suppression for professional competence. After losing Hannah, I buried my grief so deeply that colleagues admired my apparent resilience. But what looked like strength from the outside was actually a sophisticated form of self abandonment. I'd become skilled at compartmentalising my life into separate parts that never contaminated each other with the messiness of being human.

The West Point research reveals another layer of this story. Those cadets who performed best over 14 years were the ones whose motivations remained most closely connected to their work itself. When we pursue goals for too many external reasons, we actually weaken our connection to the deeper satisfaction that sustains us through difficult periods. I'd been operating with a shotgun approach to motivation, assuming more reasons would make me stronger, when it was actually making me less effective.

The car crash became my wake up call because it forced me to admit something I'd spent years avoiding. I wasn't all right. That simple admission felt terrifying at first, but it opened doors to support I didn't know existed. When I finally spoke honestly about my struggles, I finally got the help I needed.

Machine mode had served a purpose. It protected me when I was too raw to function any other way. But machines are unable to experience the true joy in life. Learning to be human again meant accepting that I could be both capable and struggling.

KEY TAKEAWAYS

1 | I stepped off the train at Euston Station with massive dreams and a heart hammering against my ribcage. Glasgow felt safe but small. London promised everything bigger. My dad wanted me close to home, but I was equally determined that moving south would absolutely be part of my plan.

2 | "We want to breed our own talent," managers would say, and my head would snap up immediately. Breed me then! I marched into HR announcing "I want to be a buyer" whilst trembling inside. They scheduled proper interviews. I passed every single one. That moment taught me how courage could actually open doors I didn't know existed.

3 | At 38 weeks pregnant, crushing dread descended. Hannah was unusually active, rolling and kicking frantically. The sonographer's expression shifted completely. "I'm so sorry. There's no heartbeat." I was preparing for birth and new motherhood chaos, not arranging a funeral for my stillborn daughter. Some illusions about control can only be shattered by reality.

4 | People at Tesco started calling me "the machine," half jokingly, half in genuine awe. I took it as a twisted badge of honour. I had absolutely no space to cry or process anything. Machine mode tricks you into thinking emotional suppression is strength, but grief doesn't vanish because we hide from it. It festers and grows until it finds another way out.

5 | The car crash happened on an ordinary weekday morning when nothing felt particularly significant until everything changed. My entire life hinged on that daily commute. When my boss asked if I was all right, instead of automatic reassurance, I croaked out the truth. "Actually, I'm not." That small admission felt terrifying but also liberating, like throwing open windows in a suffocating room.

6 | Air Force Colonel DeDe Halfhill asked her exhausted squadron "Who here feels lonely?" and hands went up across the room. What looked like fatigue was actually isolation. Brené Brown's research revealed that workplace exhaustion often masks loneliness, and sending "tired" people home alone might amplify the very thing hurting them.

CHAPTER 2

INVISIBLE ROLE MODELS

THE DAY THINGS CHANGED

"Talk to yourself like you would to someone you love." — Brené Brown, research professor at the University of Houston, author, and speaker

I remember the exact moment the words left my daughter's lips, each syllable falling like stones into still water. "Mum, I don't feel beautiful." Time shattered into a thousand sharp fragments, each one reflecting a truth I'd been avoiding. I was plunged into the hollow realisation that she was mirroring all the self-doubt I'd harboured for years but had become masterfully skilled at hiding. We were sitting in a therapy session, the afternoon light filtering through blinds. My daughter had been bright and confident on the surface, but something had been quietly unravelling inside her long before COVID-19 lockdown hit in 2020.

What made her statement so jarring was the devastating recognition that I knew intimately what that voice sounded like. The one that whispers with poisonous certainty, "You're not enough, you're not beautiful, you're not smart, you're not worthy." I had spent decades proving myself against that voice. I pushed through grief like a soldier through enemy territory, scaling corporate ladders with bloody fingernails.

And here, sitting across from me in this room, was my daughter, uttering the very words I'd whispered to myself in countless dark moments.

"She can't be what she can't see," I whispered to myself. It was true. My daughter had never witnessed me loving myself. She'd only seen me driving myself relentlessly, holding impossibly high standards for everyone around me, most of all myself. If I never showed self-compassion, how could she possibly learn it? I was teaching her, through every self-critical comment and every act of self-neglect, that women don't deserve their own love.

I looked at her, tears prickling my eyes, and thought with crystalline certainty, "It's come full circle." In that moment, surrounded by the sights of institutional carpet and the soft ticking of a wall clock, I made a promise. I would learn to love myself so she could see what was possible. I didn't have the faintest clue how to approach this mysterious "self-love" business. It was foreign territory. It was something I'd dismissed as a luxury I'd never had time for. Yet I knew with bone-deep certainty that it was urgent. For both of us.

I didn't calmly realise I needed to model self-love and seamlessly rearrange my life. The first emotion was pure panic. It felt like a bird trapped inside me. I thought desperately, "Where do I even begin?" My entire existence had revolved around external validation. I was always the "go-to" person in every job who never said no.

Coaching sessions become a sacred space to air out anxieties that had been building for months. My daughter mentioned how she managed to "spin all the plates" for so long it had become an art form. Top grades earned through sleepless nights combined with a schedule so relentless it would have crushed a weaker spirit. When the world shut down, external validation collapsed. My daughter's carefully constructed coping strategies crumbled. She could no longer maintain the mask. To her, everything felt pointless. She felt ugly and unworthy and that nobody wanted her. Little did I know that those emotions would nearly take her life before her 20th birthday.

I recognised the flat tone in her voice because it was the same monotone I'd perfected for years. When Hannah passed, I'd buried every shred of grief beneath a mountain of work that never seemed high enough. It was that numb delivery of someone who no longer believes they'll ever be enough. I'd built an entire identity around ignoring that voice and soldiering on regardless of cost. That had become my defining characteristic. But unstoppable at what cost?

When the session ended, I walked out feeling utterly rattled. Questions rang in my head. What do I want her to see when she looks at me? What's the relationship I want her to have with herself when she's my age? And how do I teach something I've never learned?

At home that evening, I sat in my kitchen and scribbled frantically in my notebook. My pen moved like it had a mind of its own. "She can't be who she can't see," I wrote. That sentence became my north star. If I wanted her to love who she was, I had to show her what that looked like in living flesh. Even if it meant dismantling the fortress I'd built around my own heart, brick by defensive brick.

I'm a natural problem-solver, someone who attacks challenges like puzzles to be solved. Once I realised I desperately needed to learn self-love, I shifted my focus entirely. My position at the time gave me access to mental health resources, coaches, and experts whose wisdom came with hefty price tags. It was a blessing that felt deeply ironic. Here I was, a successful executive in a prestigious company, yet I hadn't the foggiest idea how to look in the mirror and accept myself as I was.

I remembered an exercise an old coach had attempted with me years earlier. "Wendy, can you truly receive love?" she'd asked with the gentle persistence of someone who suspected the answer. I'd replied immediately, "Of course I can." But the moment she asked me to name three qualities I genuinely loved about myself, I froze. I could recite my achievements like a well-rehearsed presentation, but that wasn't the same as loving the woman beneath all those accomplishments.

That's when I realised I'd become a world-class expert at burying emotions so deep they might never resurface. I was exceptionally good at delivering results, but I was completely disconnected from my own heart, like a house with all the lights on but nobody home.

If I kept ignoring this part of myself, I'd keep passing that same destructive pattern down to my daughter. The cycle would continue, generation after generation, until someone had the courage to break it.

I decided that someone would be me. If I wanted my daughter to witness self-acceptance in action, I had to become living proof that transformation was possible. I had to show her that even the most broken among us could learn to be whole.

THE SCIENCE BEHIND SELF-LOVE

What I didn't know then, sitting in my kitchen with that notebook, was that my desperate scribbling was leading me towards something psychologists have been studying for decades. My instinct that self-love could be learned was backed by mountains of research that would have saved me years of floundering if I'd known about it earlier.

Scientists call it self-compassion, and it turns out to be one of the most powerful predictors of mental wellbeing they've ever discovered. Unlike self-esteem, which depends on feeling better than others or achieving success, self-compassion is something we can offer ourselves regardless of our circumstances. It's available when we fail, when we're struggling, and even when life falls apart around us.

One researcher who has been pioneering this field, Dr Kristin Neff, discovered something remarkable whilst studying how we treat ourselves during difficult times. She found that most of us have two completely different voices we use. There's the compassionate voice we reserve for friends who are hurting, and there's the brutal inner critic we unleash on ourselves.

Think about it. When your best friend comes to you devastated about a mistake they've made, you don't tell them they're worthless.

You offer understanding. You remind them that everyone struggles. You help them see their situation with perspective and kindness. But when we make that same mistake? We become our own worst enemy.

Neff's research revealed that self-compassion is made up of three essential elements that work together to transform how we relate to our own pain and imperfection.

The first element is self-kindness. When we mess up, most of us become our own worst enemy. We say things to ourselves we'd never say to a friend. Self-kindness means treating yourself like someone you actually care about. You can still take responsibility for your mistakes without shredding yourself emotionally. Beating yourself up has never made you better at anything.

The second element is common humanity. When life goes sideways, we convince ourselves we're the only ones struggling. Everyone else seems to have their act together whilst we're barely keeping our heads above water. This is an illusion. Every single person you admire has felt lost, scared, and inadequate. Your pain doesn't make you defective. It makes you human.

The third element is mindfulness. When something hurts, we either pretend it doesn't exist or let it consume us completely. Neither works.

Mindfulness means sitting with your difficult emotions without running away or drowning in them. You acknowledge what you're feeling without making it bigger or smaller than it actually is.

When these three elements come together, we create what researchers call a "loving, connected presence" with our own suffering. Over time, we learn to hold space for our struggles with the same care we'd offer someone we deeply love.

Most people panic at the thought of being kinder to themselves. I certainly did. We're convinced that self-criticism keeps us motivated and that without our inner drill sergeant screaming at us, we'll become lazy and settle for mediocrity.

The research proves the opposite. Self-compassionate people work harder, persist longer, and achieve more. They take bigger risks because they know failure won't trigger a tsunami of self-hatred and maintain the same high standards.

You'd never motivate a child by calling them worthless every time they stumbled. You'd encourage them, help them learn, and remind them that mistakes are normal. Yet we think verbal abuse to ourselves will somehow motivate us as adults.

The research validated everything I'd felt in that therapy room. Our children absorb how we treat ourselves. They watch us berate ourselves for small mistakes and learn that this is normal.

Parents who are gentle with themselves raise emotionally stronger children. These kids handle setbacks better and worry less. They grow up in homes where mistakes become learning opportunities.

The studies show that self-compassion can be learned at any age. It's not a fixed personality trait that some people are lucky enough to possess. It's a skill that can be developed through practice, just like learning to play an instrument or speak a new language.

Researchers have developed specific programmes to teach self-compassion. The results are remarkable. Even brief interventions, lasting just a few weeks, can create lasting changes in how people relate to themselves. Participants show improvements in wellbeing that persist for months after the training ends.

CULTURAL CONDITIONING

Most of us struggle to love ourselves because we've been programmed not to. From childhood, we absorb messages that make self-love feel selfish or dangerous. Understanding these hidden influences explains why treating ourselves kindly feels so unnatural.

We grow up hearing "Don't be selfish" and "Think of others first" so often that we never question these rules. Kindness and empathy matter, but when these messages aren't balanced with healthy boundaries, they create chronic self-neglect. We feel guilty every time we consider our own needs.

Women get hit with this conditioning harder than men. Society teaches us that our worth comes from caregiving and putting everyone else first. Research shows women score consistently lower on self-compassion measures across cultures. The "good woman" gives endlessly, sacrifices constantly, and carries everyone's emotional burdens whilst ignoring her own wellbeing.

I lived this for decades. Taking time for myself felt like stealing from my children or colleagues. Spending money on myself whilst my family had needs seemed fundamentally wrong. Even scheduling exercise triggered guilt because I could be helping someone else.

Modern workplaces worship exhaustion. We celebrate long hours, sleep deprivation, and constant availability as signs of dedication. Being "busy" has become an identity we wear with pride. Overwhelm signals that we're working hard enough to deserve success.

Social media feeds us a steady diet of other people's highlight reels. We spend hours daily scrolling through curated images of achievement, beauty, and perfect lives. These posts never show the failures, boredom, and struggles that fill everyone's actual experience.

Studies consistently link heavy social media use to higher anxiety and lower life satisfaction, especially among young people. The psychological concept of "compare and despair" explains how these digital comparisons systematically destroy self-worth. We're constantly measuring ourselves against edited versions of reality.

These patterns pass down through generations like toxic heirlooms. Children who grow up watching parents model chronic self-neglect never learn what healthy self-compassion looks like. If emotions were suppressed in your household or love felt conditional on performance, self-kindness feels foreign and threatening as an adult.

Attachment research shows that children develop relationship templates based on early childhood experiences. Those who received inconsistent or conditional love often become adults with harsh inner critics and persistent fear of abandonment. These patterns poison romantic relationships, friendships, and most crucially, the relationship with yourself.

Some religious and spiritual traditions, whilst offering valuable teachings, contribute to these patterns through emphasis on self-denial and suffering as virtue. Service to others matters, but when taken to extremes without balance, it creates disconnection from legitimate needs and desires. Self-care gets labelled as selfish or spiritually immature.

We can consciously interrupt these generational and cultural patterns. We can create new models for ourselves and the people who observe our lives. Self-love becomes a gentle act of resistance against systems that benefit from our insecurity and exhaustion.

When we learn to treat ourselves with kindness, we model a different way of being human. We show our children, colleagues, and communities that people deserve compassion, especially from themselves. We break cycles that have damaged generations and choose something radically different.

The voice that tells you self-love is selfish comes from a culture that profits from your self-doubt. The industries that sell you solutions to problems they helped create. The social systems that keep you competing rather than connecting.

Learning to love yourself disrupts all of this. It's the most practical rebellion you can stage against a world that needs you small. When you treat yourself with genuine kindness, you become harder to manipulate and impossible to diminish.

LEARNING TO LOVE YOURSELF

Understanding why self-love feels wrong is just the beginning. The real work happens when you start rewiring decades of conditioning through daily practice. Here are five small acts of rebellion against everything you've been taught to believe.

When someone says something nice, most of us panic. "Oh, this old thing?" we say when complimented on our appearance. "It was nothing, really" when someone acknowledges our efforts. This automatic deflection teaches your brain that positive feedback doesn't matter. Start saying "Thank you, I receive that" when someone offers genuine praise. It feels weird at first. Your inner critic will scream that you're being arrogant. Ignore it. Each compliment becomes practice for self-acceptance. You're literally rewiring your brain to recognise good things about yourself.

Generic gratitude lists don't work. Writing "I'm grateful for my family" every day becomes meaningless. Your brain stops paying attention to vague statements. Get specific. Write "I'm grateful for the way my daughter laughed at my terrible joke this morning, her eyes crinkling at the corners exactly like her father's." This specificity helps you remember positive experiences more clearly. It connects you to actual moments of joy rather than abstract concepts.

The voice in your head can be brutal. When you make a mistake, it calls you an idiot. When you struggle, it tells you to get over it. You'd never speak to a friend this way, so why accept it from yourself? When something goes wrong, try saying "That didn't go as planned, and I'm feeling disappointed. This is a difficult moment, and difficulty is part of everyone's experience." This acknowledges your pain without attacking your character.

Boundaries feel selfish because we've been taught that our worth depends on our usefulness to others. We believe that saying no makes us bad people. This is programming. Brené Brown tells a story about being asked to make cookies for a school fête. She said yes immediately, then spent the entire time regretting it and being unbearable to her family.

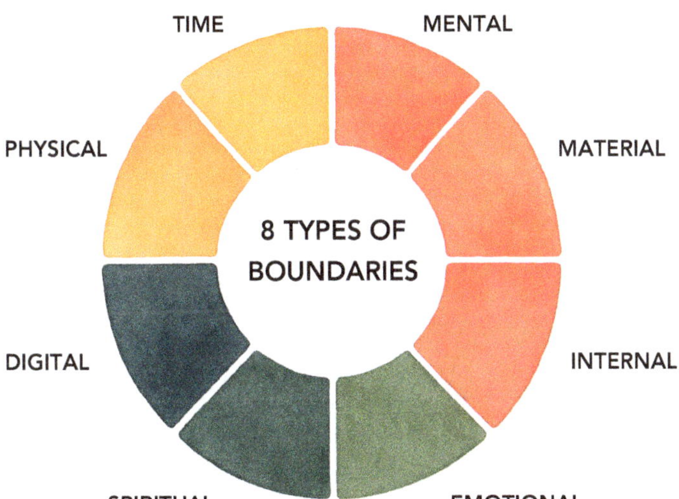

Now she spins her ring three times before answering any request, creating space to consider what she can genuinely offer. You can only give authentically when you have something to offer. Sustainable generosity requires adequate self-care. Saying no to commitments that drain you creates space for the things that matter.

Physical self-care becomes another way to beat yourself up if you're not careful. Exercise turns into self-punishment. Food becomes a source of shame. Rest becomes evidence of laziness. Feed yourself nourishing food. Move your body. Create environments that feel calm and supportive. Your body is not your enemy.

Certain emotions feel dangerous. Anger seems inappropriate. Sadness feels like weakness. Joy feels frivolous when there's work to be done. We've been taught that some feelings are acceptable and others aren't. Every emotion carries information. Anger tells you something matters to you. Sadness helps you process loss. Joy reminds you what brings you alive. Jealousy, uncomfortable as it is, shows you what you truly desire. Learning to welcome the full range of human emotion creates space for authentic self-expression and genuine connections with others.

Your brain naturally focuses on problems and mistakes. This negative bias served our ancestors well when survival depended on spotting threats. Today, it just makes you miserable. Start collecting evidence that contradicts your inner critic. Take photos of things that bring you joy. Keep positive feedback you've received. Regularly acknowledge your own progress. These practices balance your natural tendency to focus on what's wrong.

Don't try to overhaul your entire relationship with yourself overnight. Pick one or two techniques and build consistency. Small, regular acts of self-compassion create more lasting change than dramatic gestures that you can't maintain. The goal isn't perfection. It's progress. Every time you choose kindness, you're strengthening new neural pathways. Every moment of self-compassion weakens the old patterns that have kept you small.

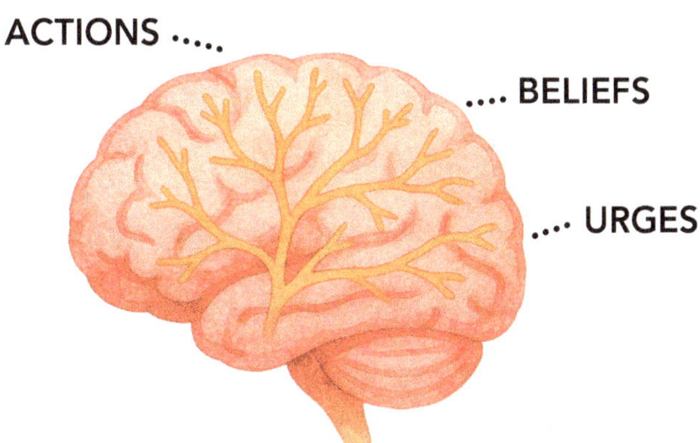

THE PROMISE I KEPT

Two years later, I watched my daughter examine herself in the bathroom mirror. She turned slightly, checking her profile, then met her own eyes and smiled. A real smile, warm and accepting. "I like how I look today, Mum," she said, catching my reflection behind her.

The promise I'd scribbled desperately in my kitchen notebook had been kept. She could finally see herself clearly because I'd learned to do the same.

The path from that panicked evening to this peaceful morning was anything but smooth. Some days I forgot every technique and fell straight back into familiar patterns of tearing myself apart. Some days the whole idea of self-love felt like expensive therapy nonsense. Some days I was convinced I was deluding myself.

But something had shifted. Those three elements I'd learned about became second nature through sheer repetition. Being kind to myself when I messed up. Remembering that everyone struggles when I felt alone. Sitting with difficult feelings without drowning in them or pushing them away. It felt like learning to speak with my non-dominant hand at first, clumsy and unnatural.

Every act of self-kindness triggered my inner alarm system. You're getting soft. You're becoming lazy. You're being selfish. Setting boundaries made me feel guilty for weeks. Fighting decades of conditioning required more energy than I'd expected.

The surprising part was watching how treating myself better affected everything else. My friendships deepened because I stopped desperately hunting for validation, and I lost those that no longer served me. My work improved because I wasn't constantly second-guessing myself. I became genuinely present with people because I wasn't spending all my mental energy managing my inner critic. The walls I'd built to protect myself had actually been keeping out most of the good stuff too. My daughter saw all of it.

None of the strategies I've shared are particularly complicated, but these small acts add up to something bigger. Each time you choose compassion over cruelty towards yourself, you're changing your neural pathways. You're breaking patterns that may have controlled your family for generations and showing everyone around you that there's another way to be human.

Learning to love yourself disrupts all of this. It makes you harder to manipulate and impossible to diminish. When you know your own worth, you stop accepting treatment that contradicts it.

This matters far beyond your own life. When you model genuine self-acceptance, you give everyone around you permission to try it too.

My daughter can be what she can see. Now she sees everything.

KEY TAKEAWAYS

1 | The moment my daughter said "Mum, I don't feel beautiful" in therapy, I realised she was mirroring the self-hatred I'd been modelling for years. Children become what they see, and she'd never witnessed me loving myself.

2 | Self-compassion has three essential elements that work together. Self-kindness means treating yourself like someone you actually care about when you mess up. Common humanity reminds you that struggle is part of everyone's experience, not evidence you're uniquely broken. Somatic work means sitting with difficult emotions without drowning in them or pushing them away.

3 | Research proves that self-compassionate people work smarter and achieve more, not less. They persist longer because they're not terrified of their own inner critic. The idea that cruelty motivates us is a complete myth.

4 | We're programmed from childhood to believe self-love is selfish. Women especially absorb messages that our worth comes from endless giving and putting everyone else first. Modern workplaces worship exhaustion. Social media feeds us highlight reels that make everyone else's life look perfect.

5 | Simple daily practices can rewire decades of conditioning. Stop deflecting compliments and say "Thank you, I receive that." Get specific with gratitude by writing actual moments rather than vague lists. Speak to yourself like you'd speak to a friend. Set boundaries without guilt. Care for your body without judgment. Welcome all emotions as information.

6 | Your brain's negative bias made sense when survival depended on spotting threats, but today it just makes you miserable. Start collecting evidence that contradicts your inner critic.

7 | This work is personal healing. When you treat yourself with kindness, you give everyone around you permission to do the same.

8 | Start small and build consistency rather than trying to overhaul everything overnight. Every moment of self-compassion weakens old patterns that have kept you small. The first step begins with how you speak to yourself in your own mind.

CHAPTER 3

FLAMINGO IN A PENGUIN SUIT

FINDING MY FLOCK

"We are the miraculous, the true wonder of this world." — Maya Angelou, poet, memoirist, civil rights activist, and author of "I Know Why the Caged Bird Sings"

At Tesco, I lived in a constant state of confusion. Senior leaders would praise my boldness one week, then make me feel like I was too much the next. "We admire how you challenge the status quo," they'd say on Monday. By Friday, I'd catch that subtle head tilt that meant "Calm down, Wendy, you're making waves again."

I felt like a flamingo trapped in a penguin suit. All that bright pink energy stuffed into black and white corporate conformity, trying to waddle in formation with everyone else. Society rewards this kind of fitting in. Don't be too loud. Don't rock the boat. Don't stand out.

I wanted desperately to belong, so I dimmed myself down. When creative ideas bubbled up, I'd offer them tentatively or wait to be asked. The irony was painful. After meetings, colleagues would pull me aside and say, "We were willing you to speak up. You had that look that says there's gold in your head."

They wanted my ideas but seemed uncomfortable when I shared them freely. I started second-guessing everything. Was I too intense? Did I offend someone? Should I have stayed quiet? The mental gymnastics were exhausting. I'd carry that tension home, never quite sure how to take off the penguin suit and just be myself.

When I heard about Salesforce's culture, I was skeptical. Their talk of Ohana, celebrating unique gifts, creating psychological safety sounded too good to be true. But I was desperate for somewhere I could finally belong.

My first week in the London office shattered every assumption I had about corporate environments. People wore funky trainers and brought genuine laughter to their work. Former retail managers collaborated with government veterans and tech innovators. Musicians had become solution engineers. The place felt like a safari of brilliant, exotic creatures.

The most shocking part was that nobody was hiding. Everyone was unapologetically themselves. I remember thinking, "Wow! This place is full of flamingos!"

Within days, colleagues were pulling me into meetings with requests I'd never heard before. "We love your energy, Wendy. Just come in and do whatever it is you do." For the first time in my career, I wasn't being asked to dim my spark. The message was "Turn it up!!"

My role was officially about innovation and building trust, showing how Salesforce technology could transform organisations. What they really hired me for was my ability to help leaders drop their armor and think differently.

I'd walk into boardrooms filled with twenty stone-faced executives from finance, IT, and marketing. Within minutes, I'd have them naming project phases after Spice Girls songs. Laughter would fill the room as formality gave way to genuine collaboration. People opened up because I opened up first.

Word spread quickly. Colleagues began physically dragging me into "war rooms," whispering urgently, "We need you in here. These folks are stuck. Go spark something."

I'd enter pre-sales meetings where teams wrestled with complex problems, only to hear someone call out, "Wendy, show us how to unlock this client's potential. You can get them talking."

I'd arrived as an unassuming innovation lead, but what I brought was a battalion of bright energy and playful methods that disarmed resistance and unlocked possibility.

The moment I truly understood my impact came during a simple office tour. A colleague from legal was showing me around when we were interrupted every few steps by warm greetings and spontaneous hugs. "Wendy! So glad you're here!" echoed through the corridors.

My bewildered tour guide finally stopped and stared. "Wendy, it's like walking through here with a rock star."

I burst out laughing. "I'm no rock star." But when you feel genuinely valued for being yourself, you radiate joy that's magnetic. Even my teenage son noticed during a visit, shaking his head in amazement as employees greeted me like a beloved friend every few steps. "Mum, this is ridiculous. You're like a celebrity."

That external recognition meant everything because internally, I'd finally stopped wearing a mask. The authenticity was real, and it translated into extraordinary results across every project I touched.

A massive weight lifted the day I realised I was truly valued for being myself. I stopped fighting my nature and started leveraging it as my greatest professional asset. That's when I truly owned my flamingo feathers.

When you're not constantly calculating how to fit in, you discover vast reserves of mental space for creativity. Psychological safety becomes rocket fuel for performance. I had more energy for innovation because I wasn't draining myself trying to be someone else.

Sometimes you are the flamingo in a sea of penguins. When that happens, don't waste energy trying to blend in. Find or create an environment that celebrates your true colors.

A flamingo never looks at its bright pink feathers and thinks, "Maybe I should tone this down." It doesn't watch penguins diving gracefully and feel ashamed that it prefers to wade.

It just exists as itself, unapologetically vibrant, and that's what makes it beautiful.

TWO TEAMS, ONE REVELATION

In 2012, Google tackled one of the workplace's biggest mysteries. Why do some teams with average talent achieve extraordinary results whilst others, packed with brilliant people, somehow never click?

They called it Project Aristotle after the philosopher who said "the whole is greater than the sum of its parts." What they discovered would revolutionise how we understand teamwork.

Julia Rozovsky experienced this mystery firsthand at Yale. Her official study group was filled with accomplished, intelligent people. Yet every meeting felt like walking through a minefield. People fought for airtime, interrupted constantly, and she always worried about saying something wrong.

Her case competition team was completely different. Members came from wildly different backgrounds but joked around, shared personal stories, and bounced ridiculous ideas off each other. When someone suggested turning the campus snack shop into a nap room with earplugs and eyeshades, nobody scoffed. They just ran with it.

This team was energising, creative, and they won their competition. The contrast haunted Rozovsky. Both groups had smart, capable people. So what made one group feel like magic whilst the other felt like torture?

When Rozovsky joined Google, she got the perfect chance to investigate. Google spent two years studying 180 teams across the company, examining 250 different factors that might explain performance differences.

They started with obvious hypotheses. Surely the best teams would have the smartest people? Maybe teams worked better when everyone shared similar personalities, educational backgrounds, or hobbies. Perhaps strong leadership made the difference, or the right balance of introverts and extroverts.

Nothing worked. No matter how they sliced the data, they couldn't find patterns that distinguished high performers. Whether teammates sat together or worked remotely didn't matter. Whether they were best friends or strangers made no difference either.

At Google, finding patterns in data is the core competency. But here, there simply weren't any obvious patterns to find. Everything changed when they stopped focusing on who was on teams and started examining how teams actually functioned.

They began studying what psychologists call "group norms," the unspoken rules governing behaviour when people work together.

Some teams had cultures where people constantly interrupted each other. Others took polite turns. Some celebrated birthdays and started meetings with small talk. Others jumped straight into business. The variety was endless, but something crucial was hidden in these patterns.

Then Rozovsky's team discovered Amy Edmondson's research on "psychological safety." When they re-examined their data through this lens, everything clicked into place.

The highest performing teams were those where people felt comfortable speaking up, sharing ideas, and admitting problems without fear of punishment or humiliation.

Project Aristotle identified five elements that separate exceptional teams from average ones.

1. Psychological Safety dominated as the most critical factor by far. When people feel safe being vulnerable, admitting confusion, or suggesting seemingly silly ideas, teams perform dramatically better.

2. Dependability means teammates can count on each other to deliver quality work on time. Trust that everyone follows through on commitments creates stability that allows risk-taking elsewhere.

3. Structure and Clarity ensures everyone understands their role, team goals, and how their work connects to bigger purposes. Without this foundation, even the safest teams struggle with direction.

4. Meaning involves whether team members find personal significance in their work. When people genuinely care about what they're doing, they bring more energy and creativity.

5. Impact is believing the work actually matters. Teams that understand how their efforts make a difference consistently outperform those that don't.

The fascinating discovery was that psychological safety mattered far more than everything else combined. Teams scoring well on other factors still showed huge performance variations, but when psychological safety was strong, everything else fell into place.

Perhaps more surprising was what Google discovered had zero impact on team performance. Office proximity, consensus requirements, personality types, individual talent levels, workload, seniority, team size, or tenure together. None of these traditionally important factors made any meaningful difference.

Matt Sakaguchi, a Google manager whose team was struggling, found Project Aristotle's results validating. The research confirmed his suspicions about why his team wasn't performing as well as other teams.

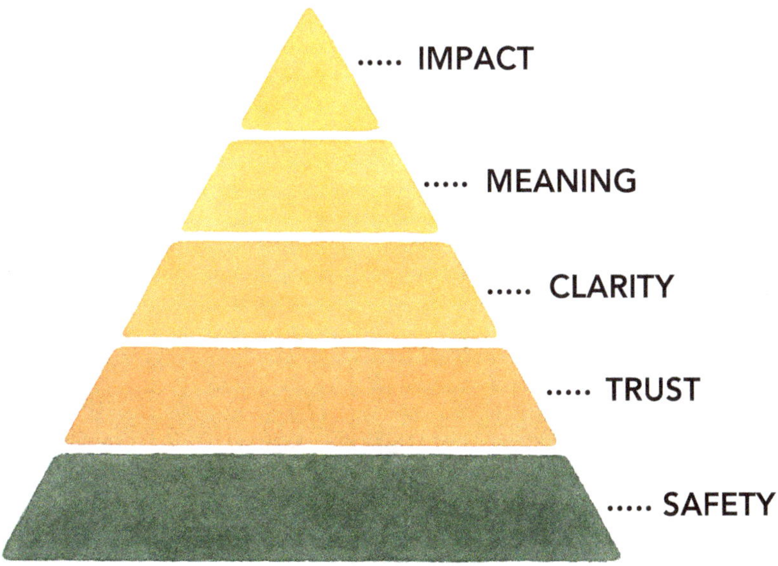

He called an off-site meeting to address their issues. To model the vulnerability the research suggested was essential, he opened with something deeply personal. He told his team he had Stage 4 cancer and his condition was worsening.

Silence filled the room. His teammates had worked with him for nearly a year without knowing about his battle. But his honesty created permission for others to share their own struggles.

By showing vulnerability first, Sakaguchi created the psychological safety that allowed honest problem-solving. They began discussing what was bothering them and agreed on new working methods.

His team transformed from struggling to thriving because they'd learned it was safe to be human with each other.

To illustrate their findings, Google's researchers described two hypothetical teams.

Team A consists of exceptionally accomplished people. During meetings, each person waits until topics touch their expertise, then speaks at length about what the group should do. When someone makes random comments, the speaker redirects everyone back to the agenda. This team is efficient, focused, and moves through business quickly.

Team B mixes managers and junior staff with varying achievement levels. People jump in and out of conversations, interrupt each other, and finish each other's thoughts. When someone suddenly changes subjects, everyone follows along. Meetings don't really end as people linger, chatting about their lives.

Most people would choose Team A based on appearances. It looks professional and runs efficiently. But research suggests Team B achieves far more.

Team A's unspoken rules discourage equal participation and personal connection. Team members can't really understand what others are thinking and feeling.

Team B might seem chaotic to outsiders, but everyone contributes. People read each other's moods and share personal information comfortably. Whilst Team B might lack individual superstars, collectively they achieve far more than their individual talents suggest.

Google's research revealed two specific behaviours shared by all exceptional teams.

First, everyone talks roughly equally over time. Conversation might not be perfectly balanced in every meeting, but by week's end or project completion, everyone has contributed meaningfully.

Second, people are skilled at reading emotions and non-verbal cues. The best teams naturally sense when someone feels upset, confused, or excluded.

These behaviours create psychological safety. When everyone gets space to speak, the first barrier to sharing ideas disappears. When teammates are emotionally aware, they're much less likely to accidentally embarrass or silence others.

When you strip away everything else, Project Aristotle reveals that the best teams are built from ordinary people who feel extraordinarily safe with each other. Once you have that safety, everything else becomes possible.

THE ENERGY AUDIT

The beauty of psychological safety is that you don't need to revolutionise your entire workplace overnight. Small experiments often create the biggest shifts. Try the "weird idea one-slide pitch." When you have an unconventional idea brewing, distil it onto a single slide with a compelling headline, one visual, and three supporting points. Then ask for five minutes at your next team meeting to share it.

This approach accomplishes multiple things simultaneously. You demonstrate original thinking without dominating the conversation. You test how receptive your colleagues are to different perspectives. You establish yourself as someone who brings fresh ideas. Most importantly, you create a safe structure for revealing authentic thinking. The key is the format itself. One slide feels manageable to both you and your audience. Five minutes isn't threatening anyone's agenda. But within those constraints, you can share something genuinely you.

Of course, nothing kills authenticity faster than exhaustion. When you're running on empty, you default to whatever feels safest, which usually means conformity. This is why understanding your energy patterns becomes crucial for sustainable authenticity.

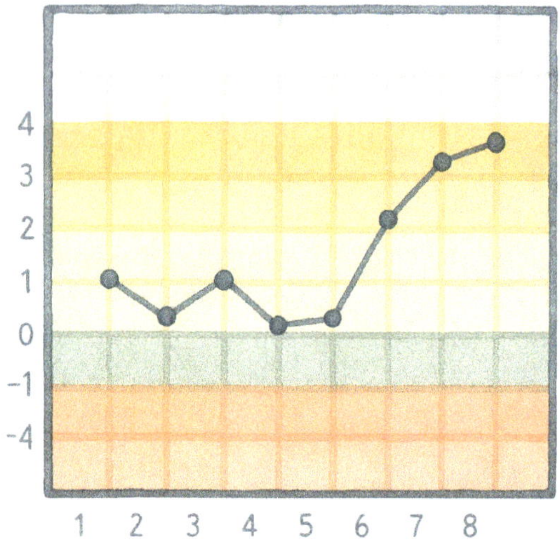

Create an energy audit over seven days. Rate every task from negative five (completely draining) to positive five (highly energising). Track not just what you do, but how each activity affects your mental state. On day eight, redesign your calendar based on this data. Delegate or batch activities rated negative three and below. Expand those rated positive three and above wherever possible.

When you operate from your natural strengths and rhythms, you contribute more value whilst feeling more yourself. Everyone wins. The specificity matters. You might discover that one-on-one meetings energise you whilst large presentations drain you. Or that creative problem-solving lights you up whilst administrative tasks feel like torture.

Beyond managing your energy, small visual cues can create psychological permission for both you and others to be more genuine. Consider adopting something that reflects your personality, such as bright socks, a distinctive pin, or an fun mug. For you, it becomes a daily reminder that you're choosing authenticity over conformity. For colleagues, it signals that individual expression is welcome. These tiny details often spark conversations that reveal shared interests and build deeper connections.

Building on this foundation of authentic signalling, you'll need to master the art of setting boundaries.

Authentic professionals don't agree to everything. They evaluate commitments against their core strengths and energy patterns, then choose where to invest fully. When declining requests, offer alternatives when possible. "I'm at capacity for detailed analytical work this month, but I could contribute to the brainstorming session where I tend to add most value." This maintains relationships whilst protecting your ability to show up genuinely engaged when you do commit.

With clear boundaries in place, you can begin practising incremental vulnerability. Professional facades feel safe, but they also feel sterile. Building psychological safety requires someone to go first in showing they're human.

Share appropriate personal interests that relate to work challenges. Admit when you're learning something new. Explain why particular projects excite you beyond their business value. This allows colleagues to see you as a whole person with interests, uncertainties, and genuine passions. When you model this kind of vulnerability, you give others permission to do the same. Before long, you've helped create the kind of environment where the best teams thrive.

This process becomes much easier when you're not going it alone. Seek out colleagues who value genuine expression and create informal partnerships that support mutual growth. Offer to co-facilitate sessions that draw on your combined talents.

Check in with each other about professional development goals. These relationships provide accountability. When you see others succeeding by being authentic, it reinforces your own confidence to drop the mask. Plus, authenticity is contagious. The more people in your environment who are willing to be real, the safer it becomes for everyone to follow suit.

As you experiment with these approaches, remember that authentic expression improves with practice, but only if you pay attention to how people respond. After each small experiment, assess what worked and what didn't. You might notice that certain colleagues respond well to your genuine communication style whilst others prefer more formality. Some meetings might feel safer for authentic contribution than others. Some projects might naturally align with your strengths. This awareness helps you calibrate future decisions.

These approaches work because they build on each other. Each small step increases your confidence. Each interaction makes the next one easier. What once felt risky begins to feel normal. Before long, you realise you're no longer performing professionalism. You're embodying it authentically. And just like Google's highest-performing teams, you've discovered that being genuinely yourself is more fulfilling AND effective.

AUTHENTICITY FLOURISHES

During my years at Salesforce, I observed fascinating leadership dynamics that revealed how organisations must strike a complex balance between culture and operations. This period taught me valuable lessons about how different leadership strengths can complement each other, and what happens when that balance shifts.

In my opinion, Marc Benioff, co-founder and Chief Executive Officer, exemplified visionary leadership at its finest. From my perspective, he built Salesforce upon a foundation of strong values and philanthropic commitments that transformed how business could be conducted. I believe his genius lay in culture-building, strategic thinking, and fostering authentic relationships throughout the organisation.

When Marc operated in his natural zone of genius, the entire company hummed with creativity, purpose, and warmth. People felt connected to something larger than themselves. The culture became magnetic, attracting talent who wanted to be part of a mission-driven organisation. This translated into real business outcomes through employee engagement and customer loyalty.

In 2018, Keith Block was name co-CEO, bringing complementary strengths that created a powerful leadership partnership. Keith's genius centred on operational excellence and systems optimisation, and execution. Where Marc inspired and envisioned, Keith organised and delivered.

Together, they formed what I witnessed as near-perfect organisational balance. Marc continued championing the human elements that made Salesforce distinctive. Keith ensured everything operated with precision and efficiency. During this dual leadership phase, Salesforce achieved remarkable success both financially and culturally. The company experienced the best of both worlds.

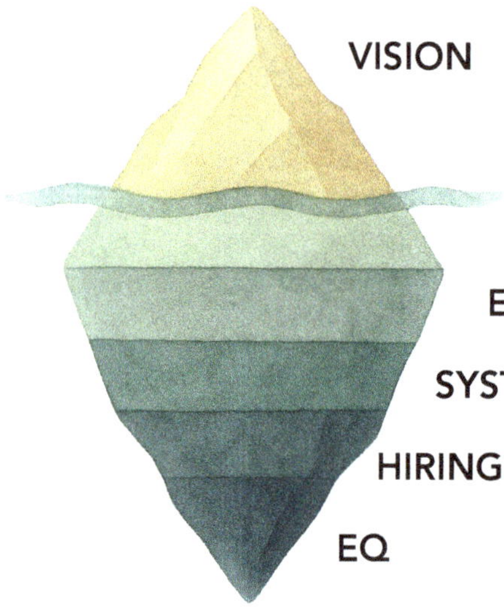

This partnership illustrated a fundamental truth about organisational leadership. The skills required to nurture culture and the capabilities needed to drive operational excellence. Although not mutually exclusive, these two functions demand different types of focus and energy. Most leaders excel more naturally in one area than the other. Attempting to optimise both simultaneously presents genuine challenges that even the most talented leaders struggle to master.

In 2020, Keith Block stepped down. When leadership structures changed, responsibilities consolidated under Marc. During this time, I observed the natural tensions that emerge in any growing organisation.

Keith and Marc were both exceptionally talented leaders. But the change highlighted the inherent difficulty of maintaining balance between visionary culture-building and operational execution within a single role.

Organisations constantly grapple with whether to prioritise growth and efficiency or culture and values. The reality is that sustainable success requires both, but the skills and mindset needed for each often pull leaders in different directions.

The operational demands of running a large, complex organisation can consume enormous amounts of time and mental energy. Quarterly targets, system optimisations, and efficiency improvements require detailed focus and analytical thinking. Meanwhilst, culture-building requires presence, emotional intelligence, and the ability to inspire people around shared values and purpose.

Around the offices, people affectionately began referring to me as Salesforce's unofficial "Chief Energy Officer." My role involved bringing intangible spark into everything, whether energising conversations with potential customers or bridging departmental divisions. I thrived on creating connections between people and helping teams see possibilities they hadn't considered.

During periods when cultural elements received dedicated senior attention, I felt unstoppable in that capacity. The organisation's commitment to values like Ohana created space for people like me to operate authentically. When leadership actively championed the human side of business, it gave permission for others throughout the organisation to prioritise relationships, creativity, and authentic engagement.

This experience taught me that culture requires active, ongoing attention. When leaders model the behaviours they want to see and create space for authentic expression, it cascades throughout the organisation. When operational pressures dominate leadership attention, cultural elements can inadvertently take a back seat, even with the best intentions.

The most successful companies often benefit from leadership teams that combine visionary and operational strengths rather than expecting single leaders to excel equally in both areas. The challenge for any growing organisation lies in maintaining this balance over time.

As companies scale, the temptation to prioritise operational efficiency over cultural elements can be strong. Quarterly pressures, investor expectations, and competitive dynamics all push towards optimisation and execution. Yet the companies that sustain long-term success often find ways to preserve both elements.

FREEDOM TO FLY

I spent years trying to solve the wrong puzzle. I twisted myself into impossible shapes, dimming my brightness to fit their mould. I was a flamingo in a penguin suit, and I thought the problem was me. Too loud, too much, and too different. I exhausted myself calculating every word.

The real problem was a culture that claimed to want innovation whilst punishing the very authenticity that creates it. They hired me for my perspective, then made me feel unsafe sharing it. The cognitive gymnastics were crushing.

Salesforce showed me what becomes possible when you stop fighting yourself. When Marc Benioff built a culture that genuinely celebrated authenticity, people soared. The energy I'd been wasting on conformity suddenly became available for truly meaningful work.

Google's Project Aristotle validates everything I experienced firsthand. Psychological safety transforms teams from collections of individuals into something special. When people feel safe to be vulnerable and suggest wild ideas, collective intelligence skyrockets.

The world needs more flamingos willing to embrace their true colours. We need authenticity because it works. It drives innovation, builds trust, and unleashes collective intelligence that solves real problems.

Your quirks are competitive advantages waiting for the right environment to shine. A flamingo never looks at its bright pink feathers and thinks it should tone them down.

Sometimes you'll find yourself the only flamingo in a sea of penguins. You can spend your energy trying to waddle in formation, exhausting yourself whilst contributing a fraction of your potential. Or you can find environments where your authentic self is welcomed and leveraged for the unique value it brings.

Changes starts with one person brave enough to shed their penguin suit and embrace what makes them beautifully, unapologetically unique.

That person could be you.

KEY TAKEAWAYS

1 | At Tesco, I felt like a flamingo trapped in a penguin suit. Senior leaders would praise my boldness one week, then make me feel like I was too much the next. I exhausted myself calculating every word and gesture, dimming my natural brightness to fit their corporate mould.

2 | Salesforce showed me what becomes possible when you stop fighting yourself. Marc Benioff built a culture that genuinely celebrated people being themselves. The energy I'd been wasting on trying to fit in suddenly became available for creativity, connection, and meaningful work. When you feel valued for being yourself, you radiate joy.

3 | Google's Project Aristotle studied 180 teams and discovered that psychological safety matters more than anything else for team performance. The highest performing teams were those where people felt comfortable speaking up, sharing ideas, and admitting problems without fear of punishment.

4 | When teammates feel safe being vulnerable and emotionally aware of each other, collective intelligence rises. Team B might seem chaotic with people interrupting and finishing each other's thoughts, but they achieve far more than the polished, efficient Team A.

5 | Small experiments create the biggest shifts toward authenticity. Try the "weird idea one-slide pitch" to test how receptive your colleagues are to different perspectives. Create an energy audit rating tasks from negative five to positive five to understand your natural rhythms. Use small visual cues like bright socks or distinctive pins to signal that individual expression is welcome.

6 | Authentic professionals master strategic boundaries by evaluating commitments against their core strengths. When declining requests, offer alternatives like "I'm at capacity for analytical work this month, but I could contribute to brainstorming where I add most value." Practice incremental vulnerability by sharing appropriate personal interests and admitting when you're learning something new.

CHAPTER 4

EMOTIONAL INHERITANCE

THE PATTERNS WE INHERIT

"I am my own experiment. I am my own work of art." — Madonna, singer, songwriter, actress, and pop culture icon

The small kitchen in our Glasgow home remains etched in my memory with painful clarity. My mother and brother would sit together on the old sofa, sharing whispered jokes and knowing glances whilst I stood in the doorway, forever missing the punchline. Their connection seemed effortless, a private world of nudges and giggles that had no space for me.

They rarely told me to leave. They simply never invited me in.

This pattern of exclusion became my first lesson in how love worked. If only I could be funnier, brighter, more agreeable, perhaps my mother would include me in her easy banter with my brother. The logic seemed sound to my young mind, love was something you earned through perfect behaviour.

My father's presence only reinforced this belief. He would return from work trips like a commanding officer, issuing instructions and reshaping our household according to his vision of proper order. To me, his micromanagement felt like evidence that he didn't trust my capabilities. Even at home, I was failing some invisible test.

I remember presenting my mother with a crayon drawing, carefully crafted lines forming what I hoped resembled our family. She barely glanced at it before setting it aside with distracted indifference. Yet when my brother waved his scribbles before her, she would dissolve into delighted laughter, praising his imagination with genuine warmth.

These moments carved deep grooves in my developing psyche. They taught me that attention must be earned, that love came with conditions, and that I hadn't yet discovered the secret formula for belonging.

The child I was learned to contort myself for love with remarkable efficiency. I did well at school, helped with household tasks without being asked, and grew quiet whenever I sensed my presence wasn't wanted. I became an expert at reading rooms, adjusting my volume and very essence to match what seemed required.

Yet no matter how perfectly I performed, the feeling of being slightly out of place persisted. This early apprenticeship in earning worthiness would shape my worldview for decades to come.

As I moved through my teenage years, my hunger for belonging took on new forms. I desperately wanted acceptance from friends and teachers, anyone who might offer an approving nod.

I studied the popular girls like an anthropologist, mimicking their clothes, speech patterns, and interests. I buried my own preferences whenever they threatened to make me stand out unfavourably.

This pattern of adaptive camouflage followed me into my corporate career, where fitting in seemed essential for advancement. I became a master of professional shapeshifting, offering different versions of myself to different colleagues, always calibrating for maximum acceptance.

The cost of this constant shapeshifting was a life lived in perpetual anxiety. I scanned every social interaction for signs of approval or rejection.

The achievements on my CV multiplied. People filled the spaces around me. Yet beneath it all lay a persistent loneliness that no amount of external validation could touch.

Years later, I discovered that this loneliness stemmed from the absence of my own authenticity. I had become so skilled at offering people a polished, carefully crafted version of myself that I had forgotten who I actually was beneath the performance.

This manufactured persona might have earned me seats at certain tables, but it couldn't satisfy the fundamental human need to be seen and loved for who I truly was. I had succeeded at becoming acceptable, but failed at becoming myself.

BREAKING THE PATTERN

My resentment towards my mother simmered for years, a low-grade fever of anger that coloured our every interaction. I couldn't shake the conviction that her emotional distance had set this painful pattern in motion. Seeking answers, I turned to family constellation therapy, a process where strangers stand in as your family members. This allows you to observe the unspoken dynamics that flow through generations.

What emerged in that session shattered my narrow understanding of our family story. I witnessed a long lineage of women weighed down by unprocessed grief, heartbreak, and limitations imposed by circumstance.

I grasped that my mother had likely learned, through her own painful experiences and family history, to keep herself carefully guarded. Where I had perceived deliberate rejection, there was also fear and bone-deep fatigue on her part.

This realisation cracked open a door I hadn't known existed. I began to understand that I could accept my mother for who she was, complete with her limitations and wounds. I didn't need to force her to become the nurturing figure I had always craved.

In extending this acceptance to her, I discovered I could offer the same grace to myself. There was room to acknowledge the hurt whilst honouring my mother's vulnerability and the fact that she had indeed given me enough.

My father's protective instincts, which had felt suffocating during my youth, also took on new meaning through this lens of understanding. When my daughter died as a stillbirth, his anxiety about losing people he loved went into overdrive. He would call incessantly, terrified that I was teetering on the edge of despair and a breakdown.

For a long time, his hovering drove me to distraction. Then it dawned on me that his method of "protecting" was the only language he knew for expressing care. He, too, had been shaped by his own story of loss and fear, wounds that predated my existence by decades.

I began reaching out to him proactively, offering reassurance before his panic could escalate. In response, he gradually loosened his controlling grip on my choices. A new respect grew between us, built on mutual understanding.

Although we never became the type of father and daughter who discussed feelings at length, we found a peaceful middle ground rooted in acceptance. We learned to love each other within the constraints of our respective emotional vocabularies.

These family reckonings taught me that if I wanted to stop feeling lonely, I needed to start by belonging to myself. This meant acknowledging all parts of my identity. My fears and ambitions. My quirky sense of humour. Even my mistakes and failures. Only when I decided that I was enough could I begin showing up in the world as myself.

The family patterns that had shaped me didn't disappear, but they lost their power to dictate my relationships. I could carry the lessons without carrying the wounds and honour my parents' struggles. When you stop contorting yourself for love, you learn that real love doesn't require contortion at all.

FINDING BELONGING

Belonging is frequently misunderstood as simply being part of a group, but true belonging operates on a different frequency. It represents the sense that you can be yourself, mask-free and unguarded, whilst still being accepted. Fitting in requires endless shape-shifting and self-censorship. Belonging allows you to show up exactly as you are, imperfections and all.

When we continuously mask our authentic selves, loneliness persists even in crowded rooms. This explains why so many people describe feeling isolated at work or at home, even whilst being surrounded by others. No quantity of surface connections can substitute.

Despite living in an era of unprecedented connectivity, loneliness has surged worldwide. Many possess hundreds of online "friends" yet have no one to call during their darkest moments. Researchers have discovered that chronic loneliness poses health risks comparable to smoking or obesity.

A 2025 meta-analysis examining data from 90 cohort studies revealed stark evidence about mortality risks associated with social isolation. The research demonstrated that loneliness, social isolation, and living alone are all linked to higher all-cause mortality rates.

Our early environments condition us to seek validation in ways that often undermine authentic connection. When we sense during formative years that love depends on performance, we internalise a "keep performing, keep pleasing" mentality.

Many workplaces reinforce this pattern through reward systems that praise those who conform perfectly, never take time off, always say yes, and meet every unspoken expectation. Over time, this hustling for approval becomes a lifestyle that leaves little room for self-expression.

The paradox becomes clear through research on self-compassion and relationship quality. Five-year studies focusing on mid-life women found that higher levels of self-compassion predict lower depressive symptoms years later. Those who struggle with self-acceptance tend to develop more severe depressive episodes over time. This research suggests that our capacity to love others authentically depends largely on our willingness to embrace ourselves.

We face a fundamental tension. The more we hustle for external approval, the more we become what others need us to be, and the less we show up as ourselves. This creates a recipe for loneliness, because real belonging cannot exist without the courage to be ourselves.

Contemporary neuroscience research provides insights into the biological mechanisms underlying authentic connection. Brain imaging studies reveal that when we witness genuine emotional expression from others, our mirror neurons activate, creating neurological empathy.

This explains why sharing struggles with friends often brings people closer than sharing successes, despite our cultural tendency to believe the opposite. When someone shares their challenges, our brains literally mirror their experience, creating the biological foundation for human connection.

Studies on vulnerability and oxytocin release demonstrate that appropriate self-disclosure changes our brain chemistry, creating biological foundations for deeper trust and intimacy. When we share genuine aspects of our experience, both we and our listeners experience increased levels of bonding hormones that facilitate emotional connection.

This helps explain why honest conversations often feel energising, despite requiring greater emotional vulnerability. Our brains reward authentic connection by releasing chemicals that make us feel good, creating a biological incentive to seek deeper relationships. In other words, biological evidence suggests that our brains are wired to crave human connection.

THE POWER OF INITIATION

For years, I hardly ever took the first step in social situations. Birthdays, holidays, even casual tea invitations all passed by without me getting involved. I would wait for other people to invite me. Part of this came from having a hectic schedule, but honestly, fear was hiding beneath every excuse I made.

What if they're too busy? What if they don't actually want to spend time with me? I preferred staying quiet and safe rather than risking the vulnerability of hearing "No, sorry" and feeling that familiar sting of not being good enough.

I genuinely love being around people. But my childhood had taught me that maybe I wasn't someone others actively sought out. So I waited for invitations that never came, convincing myself I was happy with being alone when loneliness was actually chipping away at my confidence.

It took me years to realise how deeply I had absorbed this fear of asking. When I finally started talking to other people about it, I discovered that loads of my friends had exactly the same fears. Half of them later told me they never suggested coffee dates or lunch plans because they assumed everyone else was too busy to be bothered.

I found myself encouraging them to break these patterns whilst still doing exactly the same thing in my own life. The contradiction became impossible to ignore.

So I decided to become more deliberate about creating opportunities for connection, starting with something as simple as lunch dates. I made a promise to myself to text one friend each week and ask if they fancied meeting up for a meal.

At first, my stomach would flip as I typed these messages. But I made myself press send anyway, stepping out of my comfortable but lonely bubble. The responses surprised me.

The first friend replied straight away. "Yes! I'd love that. How's Thursday?" Another said, "Oh my goodness, it's been ages, absolutely." People were genuinely pleased. Why had I been so terrified?

When someone couldn't make it, they usually suggested other dates instead. I realised I had been creating my own loneliness by never taking the risk of reaching out. As I kept arranging these casual meetups, my social circle quietly grew. Someone I hadn't spoken to in a year invited me to her house for dinner. "Next time, come over," she said. "I'll cook."

The give and take became obvious once I stopped waiting to be chosen. This shift from passively hoping to actively building community started dissolving the loneliness I had carried around for so long. People responded to the initiative with their own initiative. When I showed that I valued their company enough to reach out, they began reaching out to me as well. The social momentum built naturally from there.

This reflects a bigger change in how we see our own worth. When we wait for others to reach out, we unconsciously strengthen the belief that we're not worth pursuing. When we take the first step, we show the kind of connection we want to see in the world.

BUILDING CONNECTION

Breaking the cycle of feeling like an outsider starts with specific, practical strategies. The key lies in developing "authentic self regard," a stable sense of worth that doesn't depend on what other people think of you.

The first step involves spotting your belonging triggers. Most of us have particular situations, places, or types of people that set off our people pleasing responses. These might include family gatherings where you slip back into childhood roles, work meetings where you keep your opinions to yourself to avoid conflict, or social settings where you change your interests to seem more acceptable.

Pay attention to the physical feelings that come with these shifts. You might notice changes in your voice, or a sense of disconnecting from yourself. Understanding these triggers helps you interrupt the pattern before it fully kicks in.

Creating regular "self belonging" rituals can ground you in self acceptance. Simple practices work best when you can stick to them. Each morning, place a hand on your heart and say quietly to yourself, "I accept who I am today," or spend two minutes writing down three things you appreciate about yourself.

What you actually do matters less than doing it consistently with genuine intention. These small daily acknowledgements train your brain to recognise your inherent worth instead of constantly looking for it from other people.

Develop "value based authenticity" through activities that genuinely spark joy. Write down what makes you feel most like yourself. Then commit to including at least one of these concepts in your weekly routine. When you regularly do what truly energises you, you show up more fully in every way.

Try hosting a small gathering. Every couple of weeks, invite exactly two people for coffee or tea. The specific number matters because three people create an ideal balance.

Choose a mix of colleagues, neighbours, or new contacts, focusing on people you'd like to know better. Taking the lead in creating these small connections builds confidence whilst expanding your social circle.

Instead of asking "How are you?" try following up with "What's been the best part of your week?" and "What's been challenging you lately?" Most people appreciate the chance to share beyond surface level chat.

KEY TAKEAWAYS

1 | My childhood in Glasgow taught me that love had to be earned through perfect behaviour. Watching my mother and brother share whispered jokes whilst I stood in the doorway, forever missing the punchline, showed me I wasn't automatically included. I learned to contort myself for love with remarkable efficiency, becoming an expert at reading rooms and adjusting my very essence to match what seemed required.

2 | Family constellation therapy broke my narrow understanding of our family story. I discovered a long lineage of women weighed down by unprocessed grief and limitations imposed by circumstance. My mother had learned to keep herself carefully guarded through her own painful experiences. Extending acceptance to her allowed me to offer the same grace to myself.

3 | Belonging means you can show up mask-free and unguarded. Fitting in requires endless shape-shifting and self-censorship. When we continuously mask our authentic selves, loneliness persists even in crowded rooms, which explains why people feel isolated despite being surrounded by others.

4 | Research reveals that chronic loneliness poses health risks comparable to smoking or obesity. A 2025 meta-analysis of 90 studies showed that loneliness, social isolation, and living alone are all linked to higher mortality rates. The physiological stress of chronic disconnection appears to accelerate ageing processes, making authentic connection a literal life-or-death issue.

5 | Our brains are wired for authentic connection. When we witness genuine emotional expression from others, our mirror neurons activate, creating neurological empathy. Brain imaging studies reveal that sharing struggles brings people closer than sharing successes because our brains literally mirror others' experiences, creating the biological foundation for human connection.

6 | For years, I never took the first step in social situations because childhood had taught me I wasn't someone others actively sought out. I waited for invitations that never came, convincing myself I was happy alone when loneliness was chipping away at my confidence. When I started texting one friend each week to suggest lunch, people were genuinely pleased and often responded with their own invitations.

CHAPTER 5

HUMAN SUSTAINABILITY

BROKEN MACHINES

"Nourishing yourself in a way that helps you blossom in the direction you want to go is attainable, and you are worth the effort." — Deborah Day, author and speaker

After eighteen months of leading what we euphemistically called a "heart and lung transplant" at Tesco, one of those transformation programmes that devours everything in its path, I found myself staring in the mirror at a total stranger. Dull hair framed a face drained of colour, deep grooves carved across my forehead like worry made permanent. The woman looking back appeared twenty years older than the one who had started this journey.

But it was my husband's quiet observation that shattered my carefully constructed delusions. "We lose you to Tesco on holidays," he said, his voice carrying no anger, only the weight of accepted defeat. "You get sick, we fix you up, then we send you back. That's our life now."

The matter-of-fact delivery cut deeper than any confrontation could have. In that moment, I understood what I had become. Not the indispensable leader I imagined, but a broken machine grinding through each day whilst my family collected the pieces.

I had built my identity around titles that felt like armour. Director of Change. Programme Leader. Problem Solver. I was transforming an organisation whilst systematically dismantling myself. Machines don't require sleep or family dinners. They don't need their children to remember what they look like when they're not exhausted. They simply run until they break.

Yet there was a perverse pride in this destruction. "They can't do this without me." Our culture celebrates this relentless self-sacrifice, dressing it up in noble language, such as commitment, work ethic, and resilience. We've made martyrdom fashionable, turning self-destruction into a virtue. But strip away the corporate poetry, and what remains is self-harm in its most insidious form.

We associate self-harm with immediate, visible damage. We don't recognise the violence of ignoring our body's desperate signals for rest. This is self-harm in slow motion, a gradual erosion that feels almost voluntary until suddenly it isn't.

I recognise this pattern everywhere now. From the colleagues who compulsively accept every assignment because declining feels like betrayal to the leaders who measure their worth in outputs, as if human value could be quantified in spreadsheets. There are the parents who promise themselves "just one more push" whilst their children learn to expect absence.

In quiet moments, they all sense something fundamental has gone wrong, but the machinery of busy-ness keeps them too distracted to address it.

Burnout works like water on stone, each late night carving away another sliver of well-being. You don't notice the damage until the day you realise there's nothing left to erode.

For me, that reckoning came through my husband's unflinching honesty. He had been witnessing my disintegration. My family become my maintenance crew, patching me up just enough to send me back into the machine.

The warning signs had been screaming for months, but I had grown expert at translating distress into dedication. My body was staging increasingly desperate interventions, forcing rest through illness when I refused to choose it voluntarily.

This cycle felt normal because it was ubiquitous. Everyone around me was running the same punishing race. The compensation was good, the projects were meaningful, and my name attached to visible successes. Surely this was worth the personal cost?

Yet in all our discussions about sustainability, we systematically ignore the most fundamental resource requiring conservation. Human capacity. We speak eloquently about environmental stewardship whilst treating ourselves as infinite, renewable resources. This is foolish.

True sustainability must begin with the humans attempting to create it because without healthy bodies, clear minds, and intact spirits, our environmental efforts become theatre performed by depleted actors who lack the energy for lasting change.

RUNNING ON FUMES

Warren Buffett has this brilliant analogy that really gets to the heart of how we treat our most precious possessions. Pretend for a moment that you're sixteen years old, standing in a bright showroom, when someone walks up with an incredible offer. They're going to give you your absolute dream car, maybe a sleek Ferrari or a rugged Land Rover, completely free. There's just one catch, and it's completely non negotiable. This single car has to last you for your entire lifetime.

This car has to carry you through your twenties as you build your career, through your thirties as you perhaps start a family, through your forties and fifties as you navigate midlife challenges, and into your golden years. Every journey you'll ever take, from daily commutes to cross country adventures, from emergency hospital visits to wedding celebrations, depends entirely on this one machine.

Knowing what's at stake, how would you treat such a car? The answer is obvious. You would look after it with absolute devotion. You would study the owner's manual until you could recite it from memory. Every recommended service would be done with clockwork precision. The oil changes, transmission flushes, brake inspections, tyre rotations, and spark plug replacements.

You would buy only the highest quality parts, never cutting corners with cheap alternatives that might damage long term performance, and get to know every sound your engine makes.

The slightest unusual noise would send you straight to a trusted mechanic, because you'd understand that small problems left alone become massive failures. You would park under cover whenever possible, wash it regularly to prevent rust, and treat every component as if your life depended on it.

Now pretend for a second that it's not one car you'll have for the rest of your life, but one body. We get exactly one for our entire existence. Yet look at how most people treat these irreplaceable assets compared to their cars, and the contradiction becomes almost bizarre.

Many people can tell you exactly when their car's next checkup is due but couldn't remember their last blood pressure reading. We track our car's mileage obsessively whilst ignoring the warning signals our bodies send us every day.

We would never dream of filling our car's tank with contaminated fuel, knowing it would clog the filters and wreck the engine. Yet we routinely fill our bodies with foods that cause inflammation, send blood sugar levels through the roof, and burden our digestive systems with artificial additives our biology can barely cope with.

We already have the wisdom needed to care for our most valuable assets. We just need to apply the same careful attention to our bodies and minds that we would give to an irreplaceable car. Because unlike our cars, when our bodies and minds break down, there's no roadside assistance coming to rescue us.

THE MISSING LINK

A study across thirty seven countries reveals how personal wellbeing connects to environmental stewardship. Researchers analysed over 100,000 people and found that life satisfaction, positive emotions, and mental health independently predict pro environmental behaviour. This creates what scientists call a "double dividend" when we care for both people and planet.

The data shows that individuals with greater wellbeing engage more readily in sustainable practices, from energy conservation to community environmental projects. The research used quantile regression to examine how different factors affect people at various levels of environmental engagement. What they discovered was fascinating. People's knowledge of environmental issues had stronger effects on those already engaged in multiple environmental activities, whilst the impact was weaker for those doing fewer green behaviours.

The research suggests that when people are stressed, overwhelmed, or burnt out, they retreat from environmental issues, focusing only on immediate survival needs. The data confirms this. Sleeplessness, stress, and depression all negatively correlated with environmental action.

This aligns with my observations in corporate settings. When teams operate under relentless pressure, sustainability initiatives take a back seat. People lack mental bandwidth to consider long term goals when struggling to meet deadlines. The tunnel vision that accompanies chronic stress leaves little room for the broader thinking required to address anything else.

Companies invest millions in carbon offsetting whilst creating workplace cultures that drain employees' capacity for innovative thinking. We print "Save the Earth" posters whilst forgetting the most fundamental resource, human energy and creativity.

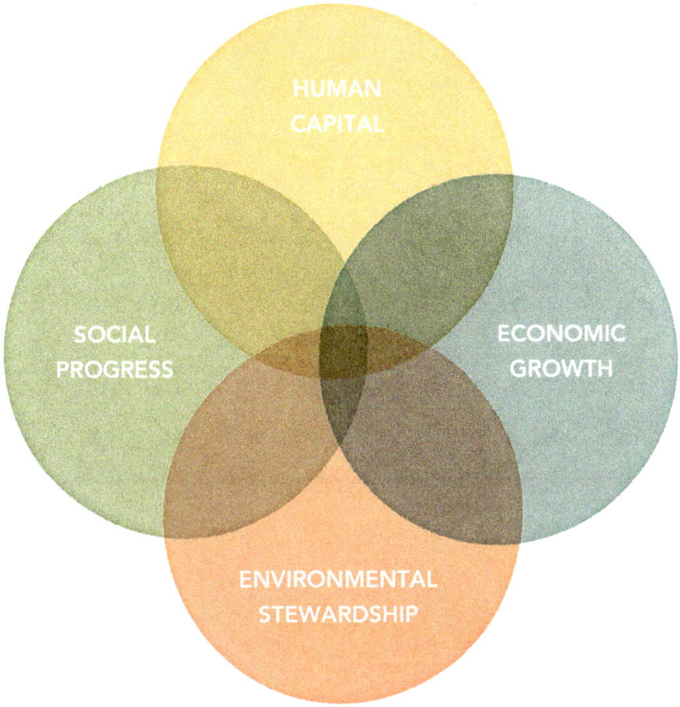

"Save the Earth" has been around for decades. We recycle, reduce emissions, and support biodiversity. Yet we overlook the humans doing the saving. If we are depleted, if our workplaces breed chronic exhaustion, how can we muster the energy needed to protect the planet?

The research backs this up. It found that people with better concentration ability, decision making skills, confidence, and sense of worth were significantly more likely to engage in pro environmental behaviour. Those struggling with overcoming hardship or feeling depressed showed the opposite pattern.

Not long ago, I was on a panel discussion on sustainability. Someone mentioned skyrocketing employee turnover. People were burning out, leaving, or staying and withering at their desks. When asked how to solve this, I replied "We cannot talk about a sustainable planet if we refuse to create sustainable people."

The room went quiet, then heads began nodding. It was a wake up call. The planet does not run on fumes, and neither should our bodies. We had become so focused on external sustainability metrics that we forgot the most fundamental resource, human capacity.

Sadly, we treat people and the planet as competing priorities rather than recognising their interdependence. Yet research suggests that the most effective environmental strategy might be systematically cultivating human wellbeing. Factors like life satisfaction, pleasure, enjoyment, and having a sense of useful role all positively predicted environmental action.

When people feel supported and have mental space beyond survival needs, they become better environmental citizens. They make thoughtful consumption choices and engage in community sustainability efforts. The research showed this pattern held across all 37 countries studied, from developed nations like Japan and Germany to developing countries like India and Myanmar.

Interestingly, the study also revealed that higher household income actually decreased environmental behaviour in some cases. This suggests that simply having more money doesn't automatically make people more environmentally conscious. What matters more is overall wellbeing and education.

These problems demand sustained effort. None of these emerge from burnout culture. We can continue treating human wellbeing and environmental stewardship as separate concerns, or we can embrace the double dividend.

EFFECTS OF SELF-NEGLECT

One night, my daughter stood in the doorway, arms folded, eyes heavy with hurt. "I never see you anymore," she said quietly. She hadn't needed help with homework or permission for anything. She simply missed her mother. Yet I was so depleted that even forming a proper embrace felt beyond my capacity. I mumbled something resembling an apology and stumbled toward bed.

Children construct their understanding of adulthood by observing the patterns we model. They absorb the toxic mythology that self-care equals selfishness and that boundaries signal weakness. For years, I showed her that human worth can be measured solely through productive output. When children witness us rising slightly earlier to savour coffee in stillness or establishing firm boundaries around work hours, they learn these choices are possible. They begin to recognise that caring for oneself forms an essential component of daily life.

Describing ourselves as "crazy busy" signals professional importance. That inadvertently teaches our children to conflate their inherent value with their measurable achievements. This messaging embeds itself deeply.

You can't save the world if you're falling apart. It sounds obvious when you put it like that, yet somehow I spent months convincing myself I was indispensable whilst my family watched me disintegrate. I told myself I was changing the world, one late night at a time. What I was actually doing was teaching my daughter that mothers disappear when work calls. The thing about burnout is that it creeps up on you like a slow leak in a tyre. You don't notice until you're stranded on the side of the road, wondering how you got there. One day you're capable and energetic, the next you're a stranger in the mirror with worry lines carved deep enough to hold small change.

I love Warren Buffett's car analogy because it's so bloody obvious. We baby our cars whilst treating our bodies like rental equipment. I know exactly when my car needs its MOT, but I couldn't tell you the last time I had a proper health check. The contradiction is almost laughable. When you're barely keeping your head above water, you haven't got the bandwidth to worry about anything else. You're in survival mode, grabbing plastic bottles and ordering takeaways because thinking about anything beyond getting through the day feels impossible. We've been approaching this all wrong. All those sustainability meetings where we talked about carbon footprints whilst creating workplaces that drain people dry.

Children learn by watching, not listening. For years, I showed my daughter that being an adult meant being constantly exhausted, that self-care was selfish. What a terrible inheritance to leave someone you love. The truth is messier than the corporate wellness programmes suggest. Real change is recognising that we've been sold a lie that we're machines that can run indefinitely and that rest is somehow weakness.

The planet runs on renewable energy. Why shouldn't we? The most radical thing you can do in our culture might be the simple act of going to bed before you collapse, saying no before you break, or treating yourself like someone you're responsible for keeping alive. Because in the end, that's exactly what you are.

KEY TAKEAWAYS

1 | After eighteen months of leading a massive transformation at Tesco, I looked in the mirror and saw a stranger. "We lose you to Tesco on holidays. You get sick, we fix you up, then we send you back," my husband said. I realised my family had become my maintenance crew, patching me up just enough to send me back into the machine.

2 | We celebrate self destruction as virtue. But strip away the corporate poetry and what remains is self harm in slow motion. Burnout works like water on stone, each late night carving away another sliver of wellbeing until there's nothing left to erode.

3 | If you had only one car for the rest of your life, you'd study the manual, do every service, use quality parts, and listen for unusual sounds. Yet we get one body for life and treat it worse than our cars.

5 | Research across 37 countries studying over 100,000 people found that personal wellbeing directly predicts environmental action. People with better life satisfaction engage more in sustainable practices. When we're stressed and burnt out, we focus only on survival.

6 | Companies invest millions in carbon offsetting. Meanwhilst, they create workplace cultures that drain employees' capacity for innovative thinking. We print "Save the Earth" posters but forget the most fundamental resource. You cannot talk about a sustainable planet if you refuse to create sustainable people.

CHAPTER 6

ARMOUR DOWN

THE FORTRESS FALLACY

"This is a moment of suffering. Suffering is part of life. May I be kind to myself in this moment. May I give myself the compassion I need." — Kristin Neff, associate professor of educational psychology at the University of Texas at Austin, pioneering researcher in self-compassion

For years, I wore resilience like armour. Colleagues marvelled at my ability to weather storms without breaking stride, returning to work days after devastating losses, maintaining perfect productivity whilst my world crumbled. "Wendy, you're incredible," they'd say, and I'd smile tightly, keeping my shattered heart hidden beneath professional competence. I believed strength meant burying pain and that survival demanded carrying on regardless of devastation.

I was wrong.

Grief taught me that unprocessed loss never disappears. It lurks in the body's tissues, feeding on suppressed emotions until it manifests as illness, burnout, or collapse. What I mistook for resilience was emotional suffocation that nearly destroyed my health, my relationships, and my capacity for healing.

When I look back at the period following Hannah's stillbirth, I barely recognise the woman I see. I switched off my grief like a circuit breaker, threw myself into my work, and carried on as though nothing had changed. There were budgets requiring oversight, teams demanding coordination, presentations that could determine our strategic direction. I told myself this was strength, that burying loss beneath deadlines demonstrated character.

"We didn't expect you back so soon," colleagues beamed. "You're a warrior for pushing through." Yet behind that stoic mask, I was disintegrating. My mind reeled with unanswered questions about why this had happened, how I was supposed to feel normal, whether I'd ever recover from losing my daughter. But I never voiced these thoughts. Instead, I buried my sorrow under forty odd emails per hour.

My calendar became a fortress against grief. Each conference call and deadline served as evidence that I was "coping well." I arrived before anyone else and left long after cleaning crews finished their rounds. The evening commute provided temporary relief because I could finally stop performing normalcy. But even then, I'd use the drive to rehearse the next day's presentations.

Nature has a way of forcing us to face truths we ignore. For me, it started with minor health annoyances. I dismissed these as inconveniences that strong people push through. But soon the minor inconveniences morphed into bronchitis and pneumonia.

I remember lying in bed, phone propped against pillows, trying to participate in conference calls with a raspy voice that could barely form sentences. In my head, I was demonstrating dedication. In reality, I was punishing a body already overwhelmed by heartbreak it wasn't allowed to process. The physical breakdown escalated gradually, then suddenly. What began as occasional sniffles transformed into persistent respiratory infections that lingered for weeks. My immune system, compromised by months of stress hormones flooding my bloodstream, couldn't mount defences against common viruses. I'd attend critical client meetings whilst running fevers, dosing myself with paracetamol and throat lozenges, convincing myself this demonstrated commitment.

Externally, I received accolades for unwavering professionalism. Internally, I was deteriorating rapidly. My sleep patterns became erratic, alternating between insomnia driven work sessions and sudden crashes where I'd fall asleep at my desk. My appetite disappeared, replaced by constant nausea that made eating feel like another professional obligation to tick off my daily list. What I didn't understand then is how our bodies react when we refuse to feel our emotions. When we keep pushing down grief, sadness, or pain, our body thinks we're under constant attack. Your stress system, which is meant to help you through short bursts of danger, gets stuck in the "on" position.

Think of it like a car alarm that won't switch off. The stress hormone cortisol keeps flooding your system, far longer and at much higher levels than it should. This wears down your immune system and creates inflammation throughout your body, like having a low grade fever that never quite goes away.

Research backs up what I experienced firsthand. When you actively suppress emotions whilst under stress, your heart works harder, your blood pressure spikes, and your whole hormonal system gets thrown off balance. Your body treats emotional suppression as a genuine threat. Even when you think you've "moved on," those stress chemicals keep circulating, triggering inflammatory reactions in your organs, tissues, and nervous system.

I became emotionally numb, unable to feel genuine joy even during happy moments. Friends started noticing how detached I seemed. My family walked on eggshells around me, not knowing how to help someone who refused to admit she was grieving.

The emotional numbness showed up in strange ways. I could talk about Hannah's death like I was discussing a failed business project. When colleagues offered sympathy, I'd quickly steer the conversation back to work, uncomfortable with any mention of my loss. I'd completely disconnected from my emotional reality. All those feelings were still there, just buried under layers of professional competence.

Every social interaction became like acting in a play. I learned to predict questions about how I was coping and rehearsed responses that would satisfy people without encouraging them to dig deeper. "I'm keeping busy" became my go to answer, followed by an immediate change of subject to work matters. This worked brilliantly in corporate settings.

Meanwhilst, everyone around me kept praising my "resilience." It felt good to be seen as unbreakable, but that image was built on a lie. Unprocessed grief doesn't disappear. It sits there, heavy and unresolved, waiting for the day you can no longer run from it.

Scientists can actually measure this. There are specific proteins in your blood that spike when you're fighting an infection. In people who suppress emotions for long periods, these same proteins stay elevated even when they're not ill. It's like your body is constantly fighting a battle that exists only in your mind. This ongoing inflammation has been linked to arthritis, diabetes, and even some cancers.

If you'd asked me whether I was mourning, I might have laughed it off. Yet the cost of denial was everywhere. My immune system collapsed, making me catch every bug going around the office.

All that praise for my "strength" created a vicious cycle. Every compliment about how well I was handling things made it harder to admit I was struggling. I'd built my entire identity around being the person who could cope with anything. Acknowledging that I was falling apart would mean destroying that carefully crafted image and letting down everyone who saw me as invincible.

The truth was, I was dying inside.

MODERN ISOLATION

We glorify "powering through," as though it's the ultimate mark of good character. Yet pushing through when your heart is shattered can quickly turn into denial. That's no longer resilience. It's suppression, and the cost to your health is enormous.

This is what experts now call "toxic resilience." It's the pressure to bounce back repeatedly whilst navigating stressful situations, without feeling able to ask for help. Unlike healthy resilience, which involves processing difficulties and growing stronger, toxic resilience demands you keep grinding no matter what, often at the expense of your wellbeing.

Modern workplace culture actively rewards this kind of emotional suppression. This manifests as employees who never take sick days and who answer emails during family emergencies. This creates environments where acknowledging grief or trauma becomes a career liability. Nearly half of young workers now report feeling stressed or anxious most of the time, yet the pressure to constantly evolve and work hard continues. When you keep pushing down grief, your brain turns into a security guard. That security guard hits the panic button, flooding your system with stress chemicals.

It’s like having a smoke detector that keeps beeping because there's a real fire somewhere, but instead of putting out the fire, you just keep taking out the batteries. Your brain starts working overtime to keep you "together" on the surface, but it stops paying attention to what you're actually feeling inside. You become really good at looking fine whilst completely losing touch with your own emotions.

This problem is made worse by cultures that still view emotional displays, particularly grief, as weakness. I grew up in Glasgow, where we hold beautiful multi day wakes on one hand, but carry unspoken expectations to keep tears from "dragging down the room" on the other. Many well meaning loved ones offer quick fixes like. "Look on the bright side," they might say, shutting down deeper expressions of grief. These responses, whilst meant to comfort, often send the message that our pain is too uncomfortable for others to witness.

The cultural messaging around grief creates impossible standards for emotional processing. We're expected to move through loss on predetermined timelines that rarely match how our bodies actually heal. "Moving on" becomes a moral duty. This creates shame around taking time to grieve properly. That, in turn, creates a pressure to "perform recovery" before real healing has happened.

Women face this pressure disproportionately. Research shows that 71% of women feel it's their job to take on the mental load both at work and at home, and 74% say they're always adjusting their lives to accommodate others. The gender pay gap, glass ceiling, and motherhood penalty all contribute to women feeling they must constantly prove their worth by never showing weakness.

The hidden grief transforms into other problems. Maybe you start getting headaches that won't go away, or you panic when stuck in traffic for no obvious reason. Perhaps you find it impossible to get close to people because opening up feels too scary. The pain you never processed shows up as anxiety, or a strange emptiness you can't explain.

Your body keeps the score in ways that might surprise you. Stomach problems that doctors can't figure out and muscle knots that massage can't fix. These might all be your body's way of expressing what your mind won't let you feel. Doctors might treat each symptom separately without realizing they're all connected to emotions you've been pushing down.

So, how do you know if you're experiencing toxic resilience? If you feel like you're letting colleagues or bosses down by not persevering, that's a red flag. If your thoughts align with a "suck it up" attitude, or if you find yourself saying "I just have to make it to this deadline, so I'm going to power through," those are warning signs. When everything feels constant and every project is "go, go, go," with endless pressure to "just push through," you've likely crossed into toxic territory.

Other signs include dreading work, feeling anxious about voicing concerns for fear of being seen as not cut out for the role, or that extreme "Sunday feeling" that's become more dreadful than normal workplace stress.

If you feel trapped in a cycle where you can't speak up for help because you're afraid of being seen as a complainer or not a team player, you're experiencing toxic resilience.

Some communities understand something many others forgotten. In certain cultures, when someone dies, the whole village stops normal life for days or even weeks to help people grieve properly.

Take traditional Irish and Scottish wakes, for example. Families would keep watch over their loved one for three full days, with neighbours taking turns so someone was always there. People would cry together, share stories, even laugh as they remembered the person. There were specific traditions that helped people express different feelings. Some involved singing sad songs to let out the overwhelming emotions. Others focused on telling stories to help process what that person meant to them.

The whole community would bring food and take care of practical needs so the grieving family could focus on feeling their feelings. It was like having a built in support system that understood grief takes time and shouldn't be rushed. Compare that with modern Western memorials, which can be quick, fleeting services. Then it's back to work on Monday without a single moment of lost productivity.

It's little wonder we struggle to process grief when our tidy timetables seldom accommodate the raw, messy process of mourning. We expect ourselves, and others, to "get on with it," skipping the important rituals that make space for sorrow.

Breaking free from toxic resilience starts with asking yourself questions like, should I be pushing this hard? Does it make sense for me to be putting this much on the line? Is this the right thing to do? These questions can help you pause and recognise when you've crossed the line from healthy coping into harmful suppression.

A 'put up and shut up' culture will never lead to effective management or productive environments.

FACING REALITY

It's one thing to realise that buried grief can harm us. It's quite another to know where to start when it comes to actually facing it. When I finally accepted that the heartbreak of losing Hannah wasn't going to vanish by itself, I felt terrified. Grief can feel overwhelming, like a massive wave that threatens to sweep you away. Yet the real danger lies in letting that grief churn inside you, creating the very chaos we're trying to avoid.

Moving away from denial meant tearing down years of carefully built emotional walls. I'd become so good at steering attention away from painful feelings that trying to access them felt like learning a foreign language. Simple questions like "How are you feeling?" would leave me genuinely confused because I'd lost touch with what was happening inside me. The numbness that had seemed like protection had actually created a dangerous disconnect from vital information about how I was doing.

When you try to "grin and bear it," the emotional parts of your brain stay fired up, continuing to send distress signals throughout your body. Meanwhilst, the thinking part of your brain gets completely worn out trying to keep those feelings pushed down.

It's like trying to hold a beach ball underwater whilst also trying to concentrate on something else. Eventually, you'll either let go of the ball or lose focus on everything else. You simply can't think clearly when you're using all your mental energy to avoid feeling what wants to be felt.

Your body has its own wisdom for processing trauma and loss, but it needs your help. The first step is facing reality without the protective cushion of denial. I had to ask myself the most basic question, "What is actually happening right now?" Whether you're dealing with death of a loved one, the end of a relationship, or major life upheaval, you have to call it what it is. This means stopping the habit of downplaying with phrases like, "It's not that bad," or, "Other people have it worse."

The words you use matter more than you might think. Instead of saying "I lost my baby," I learned to say "My daughter Hannah was born sleeping." Being direct helps your mind accept what actually happened, rather than softening it with gentle language that keeps you at arm's length from the reality.

I used to say, "I'm fine," even though I was anything but fine. Facing reality meant saying out loud, "I lost my daughter, and it's devastating." Once I could say those words, I noticed something shift in my chest, like a tiny release. It was like finally admitting to my body, "Yes, we hurt. Let's deal with it."

There's something almost magical about speaking difficult truths out loud. Even when the words are painful, you often feel a small sense of relief immediately afterwards. That's because your nervous system can finally stop using all that energy to maintain the pretence that everything's fine. All that tension you've been carrying in your muscles to keep reality at bay can start to loosen up, creating space for actual healing to begin.

Sometimes figuring out what you're actually grieving requires a bit of detective work, especially if you've gotten really good at pushing feelings away. One exercise that helped me was creating a timeline of my loss. I wrote down how I felt in the weeks leading up to Hannah's stillbirth, the hopes I'd had, numb shock afterwards, and months that followed when I buried myself in work. Seeing it all on paper helped me understand the intense sorrow I'd never actually allowed myself to voice. It was painful to revisit, but it showed me what I'd really been through.

This timeline revealed patterns I hadn't noticed before. I could see how my physical symptoms lined up with emotional milestones I'd ignored. The chronic chest infections started around the time I should have been setting up Hannah's nursery. The severe pneumonia happened during what would have been her first Christmas. This was my body's way of keeping track when my mind refused to acknowledge what I was going through.

Your body often processes emotional information faster than your conscious mind does. Learning to notice subtle changes in your breathing, how your stomach feels, and your energy levels can give you early warning signs about emotional states you haven't fully recognised yet. Your body becomes an early warning system for psychological distress that hasn't quite reached your awareness.

One practical way to honour your loss whilst creating ongoing connection is through memorial gestures. This means choosing a tangible way to remember that creates structure for grief without demanding that you "get over it" on anyone else's timeline. This might be planting a tree, making a photo book, or committing to an annual donation to a relevant charity.

The important thing is putting the anniversary or renewal date in your calendar and treating it as seriously as any other important appointment. This keeps the memory woven into your life rather than locked away.

BRINGING IT ALL TOGETHER

What I learned through my experience with Hannah's passing is that the very qualities our culture celebrates as resilience can become toxic when taken too far.

I returned to work immediately, maintained perfect productivity, and received praise for my unwavering professionalism. But beneath, my body was keeping score in ways I didn't understand. What started as minor health issues escalated into serious respiratory infections, all because I was using enormous energy to avoid feeling what needed to be felt.

When we persistently suppress emotions, our bodies interpret this as an ongoing threat. Our stress systems stay activated far beyond what's healthy, flooding us with cortisol and creating chronic inflammation. It's like having a car alarm that never switches off, eventually wearing down every system it's meant to protect.

Modern workplace culture actively rewards emotional suppression. We've created environments where acknowledging grief becomes a career liability. This has given rise to what experts call toxic resilience, where people feel pressured to bounce back repeatedly without ever being allowed to truly heal.

The cultural messages we receive about grief make everything worse. Instead of recognising that mourning is a necessary process that takes time, we're expected to "move on" according to predetermined timelines that have nothing to do with how healing actually works.

Traditional Irish and Scottish wakes were extended periods where entire communities gathered to support mourners through the messy, necessary work of grief. They recognised that loss requires time, witnesses, and rituals to move through completely. Our modern approach, with its quick services and immediate return to normal productivity, leaves people to navigate profound loss without adequate support.

Learning to move from suppression to healthy processing requires first recognising when you've crossed the line into toxic resilience. Warning signs include feeling unable to ask for help, constant "go, go, go" pressure, dreading work, or feeling trapped in cycles where expressing struggle seems impossible.

The actual work of facing grief requires you to call loss what it is rather than softening it with euphemisms. It involves paying attention to physical sensations that carry emotional information your conscious mind might miss.

Perhaps most importantly, it means finding ways to honour what you've lost without demanding that you "get over it" on anyone else's schedule.

Grief has its own timeline, no matter how much our productivity-obsessed culture might prefer otherwise.

Grief won't destroy you, but avoiding it will. The wave of emotion I was so afraid would sweep me away actually carried me toward shore, but only when I stopped fighting it and learned to let it do its work.

KEY TAKEAWAYS

1 | After losing my daughter Hannah through stillbirth, I returned to work immediately and received praise for my "incredible resilience." But what looked like strength was actually emotional suffocation. I switched off my grief like a circuit breaker and buried my shattered heart beneath forty odd emails per hour.

2 | When you keep pushing down grief, your stress system gets stuck in the "on" position, flooding you with cortisol far longer than it should. It's like having a car alarm that won't switch off. Scientists can measure this through specific proteins in your blood that spike when you're fighting infection. In people who suppress emotions long term, these same proteins stay elevated even when they're not ill.

3 | What started as minor sniffles transformed into persistent respiratory infections lasting weeks. My immune system, compromised by months of stress hormones, couldn't mount defences against common viruses. I'd attend client meetings whilst running fevers, convincing myself this demonstrated commitment.

4 | Modern workplace culture actively rewards emotional suppression through employees who never take sick days and answer emails during family emergencies. This creates what experts call "toxic resilience" where people feel pressured to bounce back repeatedly without ever being allowed to truly heal. Nearly half of young workers now report feeling stressed or anxious most of the time.

5 | Traditional Irish and Scottish wakes understood something we've forgotten. Families would keep watch for three full days with neighbours taking turns. People would cry together, share stories, even laugh whilst remembering the person. The whole community brought food and handled practical needs so grieving families could focus on feeling their feelings. Compare that with modern memorials followed by returning to work on Monday without a moment of lost productivity.

6 | Learning to face reality meant tearing down years of carefully built emotional walls. Simple questions like "How are you feeling?" left me genuinely confused because I'd lost touch with what was happening inside me. The numbness that seemed like protection had created dangerous disconnection from vital information about how I was doing.

7 | The words you use matter more than you think. Instead of saying "I lost my baby," I learned to say "My daughter Hannah was born sleeping." Being direct helps your mind accept what actually happened.

CHAPTER 7

BREAKING THE STIGMA

TRUST YOUR GUT

"When we speak, we are afraid our words will not be heard or welcomed. But when we are silent, we are still afraid. So it is better to speak." — Audre Lorde, poet and essayist

The memory of 2005 sits in my chest like a stone. That was the year I said yes when every fibre of my being screamed no. A senior leader at Tesco approached me with what appeared to be a career defining proposition. "Name your price, Wendy, and come fix our next big programme. The team expects Tesco Direct by Q4." The words carried the weight of expectation and prestige that makes ambitious hearts race.

I should have been flattered. Instead, I felt sick.

I had just emerged from a gruelling transformation project that had rewired every corner of a major corporation. The work had been relentless and consuming, leaving me mentally and physically depleted. My body was pleading for rest. Yet here was someone dangling what appeared to be a golden ticket.

The rational part of my brain recognised this as an exceptional opportunity. The deeper, wiser part of me knew it would destroy me.

Fear won the internal battle. Not fear of the work itself, but fear of what declining might mean for my future. I worried that saying no would mark me as someone who lacked ambition and couldn't handle the demands of senior leadership. Having recently secured my place at the executive table as one of the few women in that space, I felt terrified that refusal would be interpreted as weakness.

So I played what I thought was a clever game. I quoted an exorbitant fee, expecting them to balk and release me from the hook I'd accidentally impaled myself upon. When they accepted without hesitation, I knew I was in serious trouble.

The nightmare that followed taught me about the cost of ignoring our inner compass and the systems that profit from our self neglect. Tesco Direct needed to launch within eleven months. The timeline that was ambitious to the point of recklessness. The share price depended on us meeting that deadline. Leadership had staked their reputations on success. Failure, we were told repeatedly, was not an option.

Between you and me, the project was brutal. My migraines intensified. I drifted away from everything that had previously nourished my soul. Even my morning coffee, once a cherished ritual of pleasure, became overshadowed by the day's mounting anxieties. I remember standing before my bathroom mirror at five o'clock one Saturday morning, preparing for another "war room" session, and thinking with genuine bewilderment, "Who are you anymore?"

That year spiralled into some of the heaviest burnout I've ever experienced. By the time we limped across the finish line and achieved our Q4 launch, I was so depleted that no celebration felt meaningful. The worst part was the recognition that I had betrayed myself. I ignored every internal alarm to please people who would have replaced me without hesitation.

Looking back, I see this story as emblematic of a particular kind of corporate machine that treats humans as replaceable components. Tens of thousands of employees function like gears in a vast mechanism, spinning in perfect synchronisation to keep the enterprise moving forward. When any gear shows signs of wearing down, the solution is swift replacement.

Such cultures reward the relentless yes, particularly from people known for delivering impossible results under impossible circumstances. They inflate your sense of indispensability until your well-being collapses under the weight of expectations. You keep pushing forward, driven partly by pride but mostly by terror. The terror that pausing will mark you as weak, insufficiently committed to shared goals.

The machine doesn't pause for mental health. Share prices, brand reputation, and organisational momentum continue their relentless forward motion regardless of your suffering.

When you do find the courage to whisper "I'm struggling," you risk being quietly moved aside for someone who hasn't yet learned the cost of saying yes to everything. I wish I'd had the courage to say no. Perhaps I would have disappointed some executives. They may have found someone else eager to take on the job. At least I would have saved myself from a year of devastating exhaustion that compromised my health.

If I'd felt safe to prioritise my wellbeing back then, I would have done so without hesitation. The tragedy is that such safety remains elusive in many workplace cultures. We continue to sacrifice our humanity on the altar of productivity, mistaking self destruction for dedication. Sometimes the most courageous thing you can do is disappoint others to remain faithful to yourself.

WHY BEING YOURSELF WORKS

There's hard science explaining why authenticity unlocks performance in ways that conformity never can. When you can be genuinely yourself at work, your brain stops wasting energy on what psychologists call "impression management." You're no longer calculating every word, monitoring every gesture, or second-guessing every contribution. That mental energy gets redirected where it belongs, solving problems and creating value.

Research shows that psychological safety ranks as the second most important workplace factor for employees, right behind regular pay rises. When people feel safe to express themselves, team performance skyrockets. Amy Edmondson's studies prove that psychological safety predicts team effectiveness better than any other factor.

The numbers are striking. Teams with high psychological safety outperform others on complex tasks by significant margins. When employees rate their psychological safety highly, collective intelligence increases measurably. Everyone gets smarter when nobody has to hide. Modern workplaces create what researchers call "telepressure," the compulsive need to respond instantly to emails and messages.

Over half of working professionals struggle to disconnect from work during personal time. This always-on culture forces people to perform versions of themselves that aren't sustainable.

When you're constantly performing a role that doesn't fit, your nervous system treats it as a threat. Brain scans show increased activity in areas linked to danger detection and social monitoring. You're literally on high alert all day, which explains why pretending to be someone else feels so exhausting.

The contrast with authentic expression is remarkable. When people operate genuinely, brain activity shifts to regions associated with creativity and intrinsic motivation. Threat detection areas calm down. This neurological shift explains why being yourself feels energising.

Authenticity spreads. Positive emotions are contagious, moving through teams faster and lasting longer than negative ones. When you bring genuine energy to work, others pick up on it through your body language, voice tone, and interaction style. Colleagues start associating working with you with feeling more confident and willing to contribute their own ideas. This happens below conscious awareness but creates real changes in team dynamics. One person's willingness to be authentic gives others permission to do the same. Before long, you've created a culture where people can focus on their actual work.

Researcher Mihaly Csikszentmihalyi discovered that peak performance occurs in "flow states," when people operate within their natural capabilities whilst facing appropriate challenges. Authentic expression increases the likelihood of flow because it aligns work with genuine strengths and interests. During flow states, people lose track of time, feel deeply engaged, and produce their best work. Performance feels effortless because you're working with your nature instead of against it. This explains why my Salesforce experience felt so different from everywhere else.

Organisations that embrace authenticity see measurable results. Companies implementing strengths-based approaches achieve 40% higher employee engagement and 26% better performance outcomes. They also see 31% lower turnover rates, which saves enormous costs in recruitment and training. When people operate from genuine strengths, they produce higher quality output whilst requiring less management oversight. They're more innovative because they're not afraid to share unconventional ideas. They're more resilient because they're not constantly fighting themselves.

Despite individual goodwill, many organisations still require conformity. They inadvertently create systems that exhaust people whilst limiting their potential. The cognitive load of constantly fitting in leaves little mental energy for actual work.

Salesforce's culture actively encouraged people to bring their whole selves to work. This created conditions where natural strengths could flourish. The result was an environment where being authentic felt safe, even rewarded.

When organisations demand conformity, they're asking people to operate against their natural wiring. This creates chronic stress that shows up in reduced creativity, increased burnout, and higher turnover. People spend their days managing impressions instead of delivering value.

For years, my flamingo feathers were my greatest competitive advantage, just waiting for the right environment to shine. I was just too blind to see it.

ESCAPING TOXIC PATTERNS

Learning to spot toxic work environments is your first line of defence against systems that normalise destruction. These cultures often disguise harmful practices as business necessities, making their destructive patterns feel like standard professional requirements. Understanding the warning signs helps you make informed decisions about protecting yourself and finding better career paths. Toxic workplaces have several telltale signs that reveal their fundamental disregard for human sustainability. The most obvious red flag is the expectation of constant availability. Responding to emails within minutes becomes an unspoken requirement, regardless of whether it's 11pm or a Sunday morning. Weekend work transforms from an occasional necessity into routine expectation. Holidays are treated as inconveniences that committed employees wouldn't dare take.

The language these environments use often borrows heavily from military or emergency contexts, even when the actual work involves routine business operations. Teams become "troops," challenging projects happen in "war rooms," and normal market pressures get framed as "battles" requiring total commitment. This word choice creates a false life or death stakes that make questioning the pace or workload seem treasonous.

Leadership behaviour in toxic workplaces consistently models and rewards destructive patterns. When employees try to establish reasonable boundaries or request manageable workloads, they face subtle suggestions that they lack proper commitment or hunger for success.

These environments develop elaborate justification systems that make excessive demands appear noble. Unrealistic deadlines become "stretch goals" designed to foster personal growth. Constant pressure transforms into "high performance culture" that separates committed people from merely competent ones. Burnout symptoms get rebranded as temporary challenges that strong individuals push through.

Relationships outside work suffer under these conditions. Family gatherings get missed or attended with fragmented attention focused on work devices. Friendships fade as social commitments are repeatedly cancelled for professional obligations. Even romantic partnerships struggle when one person becomes chronically unavailable and perpetually stressed.

The tragedy is that these sacrifices rarely produce the career benefits they promise. Research consistently shows that overworked employees make more mistakes and deliver lower quality output than well rested ones. The apparent productivity gains from excessive hours are largely an illusion.

If you recognise your workplace in these descriptions, you face important but challenging decisions. The first option involves working within existing systems to create protective spaces for yourself and potentially others.

The second approach involves trying to influence positive change within the organisation. This requires careful strategic thinking about presenting wellbeing initiatives in terms that resonate with business focused leadership. The key often lies in framing these changes as performance optimisation strategies backed by solid research versus a touchy feely wellness program.

The third option, sometimes the only realistic one, involves recognising when a workplace culture is fundamentally incompatible with your health and beginning to plan an exit strategy. This decision shouldn't be made lightly, particularly in competitive job markets, but sometimes protecting your wellbeing requires accepting that certain environments are too toxic to reform from within.

Whatever path you choose, remember that shame around prioritising your wellbeing is artificially imposed by systems that benefit from your self neglect. Your need for rest, boundaries, and life outside work is a fundamental human requirement that healthy organisations respect and support as essential to sustainable performance.

YOUR INNER COMPASS

The years since my 2005 breakdown have brought significant growth, yet I still occasionally catch myself sliding into old patterns of overcommitment or dismissing my intuition. It's like muscle memory. The default tendency is to power through at my own expense. However, I've become far more attuned to the signals from both my body and heart that whisper, "Stop. This isn't right for you."

A recent experience crystallised how much this awareness has developed. I needed an Operations Director for my business, someone to handle the behind the scenes work that kept expanding beyond my capacity. After an extensive search, I found a candidate who appeared perfect on paper. Her credentials were impressive, my team was enthusiastic, and after decades of corporate experience, I thought I'd discovered the ideal missing piece.

From our first interaction, however, something in my gut felt deeply unsettled. She had a habit of commandeering conversations and speaking for me in ways that didn't align with my voice or values. These behaviours were subtle initially but became more pronounced with each encounter. A dismissive comment here, an assumption about my preferences there.

Red flags were appearing, yet I kept brushing them aside with rational justifications. "She's brilliant, perhaps I'm overthinking this. I need her skill set, stop being so particular." The old pattern of minimising my needs was re-emerging, overshadowed by fear of disappointing people or missing out on someone who might be perfect despite these concerns. On the eve of her planned start date, my intuition was screaming its objection with such intensity that I could no longer ignore it.

During a conversation with my coach, she asked a deceptively simple question. "How do you feel about this woman?" Not think, feel. My heart was churning with resistance, sending an unmistakable message that resonated through my entire being. "She is not your person."

The phone call I made next required every ounce of courage I could muster. I wanted to take the cowardly route of text or email, but knew that would violate my own values about difficult conversations. So I called, stomach knotted, feeling genuine physical pain because I despise disappointing people. "I'm truly sorry, but this isn't right for me."

My whole body ached with guilt for several days, reminding me painfully of how I used to ignore my needs. But the difference this time was that my exhaustion lasted a week versus before where it lasted a year. Once it passed, I felt tremendous relief. Choosing temporary discomfort saved me from months or years of trying to force a partnership that was fundamentally misaligned. If I'd overridden my instincts to avoid disappointing this person, I would have spent enormous energy trying to make something work that was broken from the very beginning.

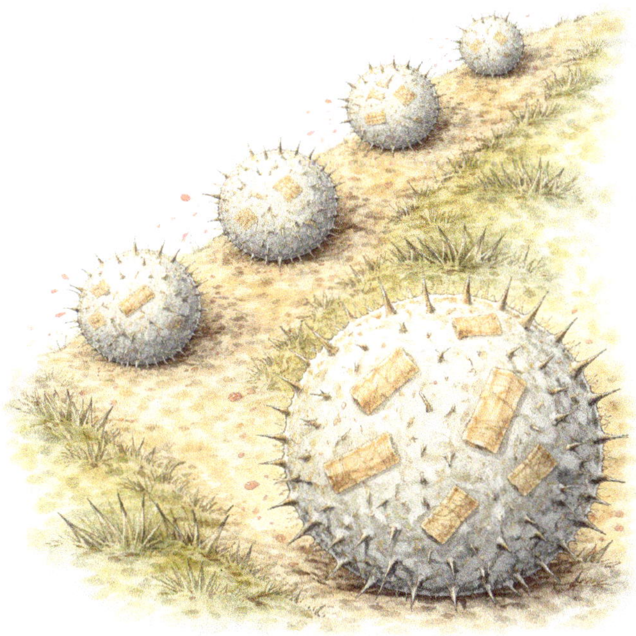

This experience illuminated a crucial truth about boundary setting that many people struggle to accept. The discomfort of honouring your intuition is always temporary, whereas the consequences of ignoring it compound exponentially over time. When we override our instincts to avoid disappointing others or missing opportunities, we often trap ourselves in situations that drain our energy and compromise our effectiveness for extended periods.

The paradox of authentic living is that by being more selective about what you say yes to, you become infinitely more valuable in the areas where you do engage.

SUSTAINABLE CHANGE

This section provides sophisticated tools for both personal protection. These approaches recognise that individual boundaries become exponentially more effective when combined with efforts to shift broader workplace cultures.

The Traffic Light Consent Map is one of the most powerful techniques for developing boundary awareness. This approach involves conducting a comprehensive audit of your regular tasks, responsibilities, and commitments, then categorising each using a simple colour coding system that immediately reveals where your energy is being well used.

Green tasks are those that energise you, align with your values and strengths, and leave you feeling fulfilled. These might include creative projects that challenge you in positive ways or responsibilities that provide genuine learning opportunities. Green tasks often have a quality of flow where time passes quickly and you feel fully engaged and present.

Amber tasks are tolerable but tiring. These responsibilities might be routine administrative work that's necessary but uninspiring, or projects that don't align with your core interests. Amber tasks represent the necessary neutral work that forms part of most professional roles.

Red tasks are energy vampires. This might include work with difficult people who don't respect your input, projects that feel misaligned with your values, or tasks requiring you to operate constantly in areas where you lack either skill. Red tasks often generate dread and may trigger physical stress responses like tension headaches.

Once you've mapped your responsibilities using this framework, identify one Red task each week that you can either eliminate entirely, renegotiate to make more tolerable, or delegate to someone for whom it might represent a Green or Amber task. This creates space for more fulfilling work whilst preventing the accumulation of resentment that leads to burnout.

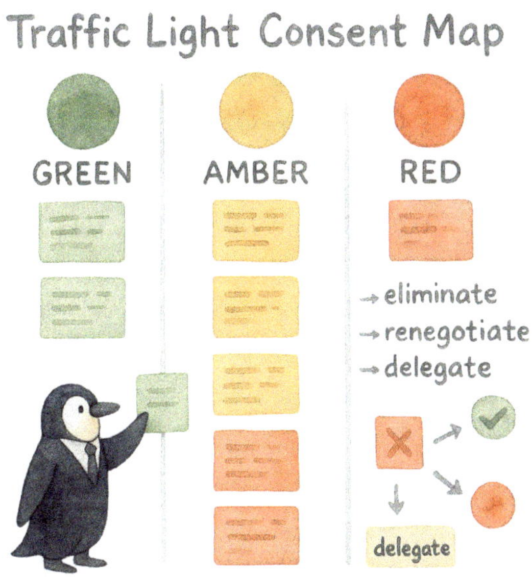

Instead of saying "I hate doing this," you can say "This sits in my Red zone, so I'd like to explore whether we can restructure it or find someone for whom it might be a better fit." The exact words matter less than developing a consistent habit of never responding immediately to requests for your time or energy.

The reflexive yes destroys more careers than almost any other workplace habit. Many people, particularly high achievers wanting to be seen as capable, automatically agree to requests before properly considering their capacity or genuine interest.

Individual boundary setting becomes exponentially more effective when supported by institutional changes that make boundary respecting behaviour the default. This involves identifying specific policy changes that would improve wellbeing across your team, then crafting formal proposals for implementation.

Rather than suggesting "better work life balance," you might propose "meeting free Wednesdays from 2pm to 5pm to allow for focused work," or "twenty four hour response time standards for non urgent communications."

When crafting these proposals, acknowledge potential concerns. If proposing communication curfews, address how urgent issues will be handled. If suggesting meeting limitations, provide alternative collaboration strategies.

I think about my 2005 self often. I want to tell that young woman that saying no is an ok thing to do. The projects I feared losing by setting boundaries were often the ones that would drain me so completely I'd become unable to contribute more meaningfully to anything else.

KEY TAKEAWAYS

1 | In 2005, Tesco offered me a career defining opportunity to launch Tesco Direct by Q4. Every fibre of my being screamed no. I'd just emerged from a gruelling transformation project that left me mentally and physically depleted. But fear won the internal battle. I worried that saying no would mark me as lacking ambition. So I played a clever game and quoted an exorbitant fee, expecting them to balk. When they accepted without hesitation, I knew I was in serious trouble.

2 | That year spiralled into some of the heaviest burnout I've ever experienced. My migraines intensified. I drifted away from everything that nourished my soul. Even my morning coffee became overshadowed by mounting anxieties. I remember standing before my bathroom mirror at five o'clock one Saturday morning, preparing for another "war room" session, thinking "Who are you anymore?" The worst part was recognising that I had betrayed myself.

3 | When you're constantly performing a role that doesn't fit, your nervous system treats it as a threat. Brain scans show increased activity in areas linked to danger detection. You're literally on high alert all day, which explains why pretending to be someone else feels so exhausting.

4 | Toxic workplaces have telltale signs. Constant availability becomes an unspoken requirement. Weekend work transforms from occasional necessity into routine expectation. Holidays are treated as inconveniences. Language borrows from military contexts even for routine business operations. Teams become "troops," projects happen in "war rooms," and normal market pressures get framed as "battles" requiring total commitment.

5 | The Traffic Light Consent Map categorises tasks using simple colour coding. Green tasks energise you and align with your values. Amber tasks are tolerable but tiring. Red tasks are energy vampires that generate dread and trigger stress responses. Once you've mapped your responsibilities, identify one Red task each week to eliminate, renegotiate, or delegate to someone for whom it might be a better fit.

6 | Never respond immediately to requests for your time or energy. The 24 hour rule prevents the reflexive yes that destroys more careers than almost any other workplace habit. Simple phrases like "Let me check my capacity and get back to you" create space for thoughtful decision making instead of automatic agreement driven by people pleasing.

CHAPTER 8

SMALL TOOLS & RITUALS

SHIFTING DIRECTIONS

"Work begets work. Small actions lead us to the larger movements in our creative lives. Take one small daily action instead of indulging in the big questions." — Julia Cameron, author of "The Artist's Way"

I used to believe the only way to solve life's bigger problems was to barrel straight through them. I was juggling work deadlines, childcare, and a lingering sense of grief that kept creeping into my evenings. I was exhausted yet wired at the same time, as though my brain were stuck in a never ending spin cycle.

Late one Tuesday, after sending my children to bed, I realised I hadn't felt present all day. I'd answered emails on my phone in the car park whilst waiting for their activities to finish and shoved some dinner into the microwave but barely tasted it. My head was so crowded with "what ifs" and leftover worry from the day that I couldn't settle. Every time I tried to relax, my mind insisted on spinning a thousand new possible scenarios. What if the finances at home unravelled? What if I'd made an unforgivable mistake at work?

These thoughts churned relentlessly through my consciousness, each one feeding the next in an endless spiral of anxiety. I lay in bed, wide awake, feeling my pulse race over absolutely nothing at all. It was as if I were running a marathon in place, shattered from the effort but not moving forward.

The clock ticked on. Midnight came, then one in the morning, still no rest. The next day, I dragged myself up and out of bed, anxious, quietly certain this wasn't sustainable.

A few weeks later, I finally shared my struggles with my coach. She listened intently, then asked, "Wendy, have you ever tried coming out of your head and dropping into your body?" I laughed. Drop into my body? In my mind, feelings were unpredictable. Certainly not the place where logic thrived.

I'd spent so many years solving problems with my intellect that the idea of slowing down to feel them felt naive. Yet I also knew the usual approach, thinking my way out, wasn't working anymore.

My head, as busy as it was, wasn't actually who I was. It was simply a receiver picking up bits of old programming that I'd never consciously updated. If I kept letting that old software play on repeat, I'd stay stuck in the same looping story. I started to wonder whether I could learn to quiet my racing mind long enough to hear what I genuinely needed.

Looking back, I see that I needed a handful of small, accessible practices to help me stay present. My mind required rituals that would let me tune in, breathe, and rewire my fraying nerves. Sometimes the biggest changes creep in through tiny daily habits.

SCIENCE OF SMALL CHANGES

We live in a culture that's crazy about change. Everyone wants the miracle diet, life changing workout routine, and revolutionary business strategy that will rocket them to success overnight. But the biggest transformation in our lives rarely come from big changes. They emerge quietly from tiny, seemingly pointless actions that we repeat day after day. There's fascinating science behind why this works, and it reveals something that goes against everything we think we know. Small habits have this incredible power to reshape our entire lives, but they do it by sneaking past us.

When we try to make massive changes, our brains basically flood us with doubt and fear and this overwhelming urge to run back to what feels safe and familiar. But when we start really small and with intention, we slip right past all those psychological alarm bells. Think about what actually happens in your brain when you form a habit. Every single time you repeat a behaviour, you're carving deeper pathways in your mind. Eventually these pathways become so well worn that the behaviour just runs automatically. You don't even have to think about it anymore. That's why you can drive home from work whilst planning what to cook for dinner. Your brain has turned these actions into efficient, unconscious routines.

Doing one push up every morning uses exactly the same habit forming mechanisms in your brain as doing fifty. The difference is in the psychological momentum each approach creates. One push up feels doable. It's almost laughably easy. Fifty push ups feels like climbing Mount Everest.

Every single action you take is like casting a vote for the kind of person you want to be. When you do that one push up, you're voting for being the type of person who doesn't skip workouts. When you read one page of a book, you're voting to be a reader. These votes add up over time, and they gradually shift the story you tell yourself about who you are.

After weeks or months of these tiny consistent actions, you stop thinking of yourself as someone who's trying to exercise and start thinking of yourself as someone who exercises. This shift in identity becomes incredibly powerful because once you genuinely believe you're a certain type of person, acting in line with that identity feels completely natural. You're not forcing yourself anymore.

Behavioural psychology research backs this up again and again. People who see themselves as helpful will volunteer their time. The behaviour flows naturally from the identity, not the other way round. This is why focusing only on results often fails miserably. We're trying to change what we do without changing the underlying story we tell ourselves about who we are.

Bad habits usually feel great right now but hurt us later. That doughnut tastes absolutely delicious in this moment, but it's quietly contributing to health problems months or years down the line. Good habits are typically the exact opposite. They require effort now but pay off later. Going to the gym feels like hard work today, but it builds strength and energy over time.

Our brains evolved to grab immediate rewards rather than wait for future ones. This made perfect sense for our ancestors who needed to food or shelter to survive. But in our modern world, this same mental wiring often works against us. We struggle to stick with habits that require us to sacrifice something now for a benefit later.

Small habits, according to author James Clear, help solve this problem by making the immediate cost almost nothing whilst keeping the long term benefit intact. Instead of committing to an hour at the gym, you commit to putting on your workout clothes. The starting point becomes so manageable that your initial resistance practically vanishes, but you're still moving in the direction you want to go.

Most of our daily routines are made up of tiny decisive moments that determine everything that follows. You either prepare a healthy meal or order takeaway. You either go for a walk or collapse onto the sofa. These micro decisions last just seconds, but they often shape how the next few hours play out.

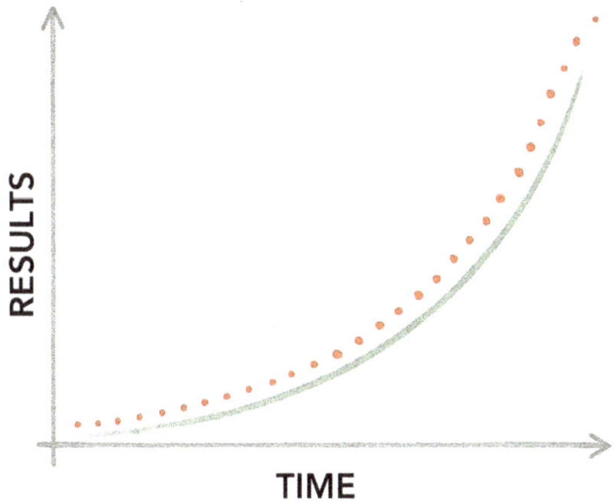

Your environment makes small habits either much easier or much harder. Your surroundings are constantly shaping your behaviour, usually without you even realising it. Put a bowl of apples on your kitchen counter and you'll probably eat more fruit. Unsubscribe from those tempting retail emails and you'll spend less money on things you don't really need.

The brilliant thing about designing your environment this way is that it makes good choices easier and bad choices harder without requiring any ongoing willpower from you. Instead of relying on motivation to resist temptation, you simply remove the temptation from your life.

Small habits work because they align with how our brains actually operate rather than how we think they should operate. They tap into our natural desire for consistency.

THE TINY CHANGE TOOLKIT

Now that we understand why small habits work so powerfully, let's look at some specific practices you can actually use. I've collected these techniques over years of experimenting with what genuinely works in real life. Each one takes less than a minute, fits into the busiest day, and creates those neural pathways we talked about earlier.

The Cold Water Wake Up Call

You know that feeling when your brain turns to cotton wool around three in the afternoon? Most of us reach for coffee or try to push through the fog, but there's something much more effective sitting right there in your bathroom sink. Walk to the nearest sink and splash cold water on your face and wrists for about ten seconds. Focus on your temples and the insides of your wrists, where your pulse points are. Then take five slow, deliberate breaths and notice what happens.

The cold water will jolt your nervous system awake in a completely different way than caffeine. It activates your vagus nerve, which is like your body's natural reset button. You get immediate alertness without the jitters or the crash later. Plus, unlike that fourth cup of coffee, it won't keep you awake at midnight.

The beautiful thing about this practice is that it teaches your nervous system to be more flexible. You're giving yourself a controlled bit of stress and then consciously recovering from it. This transfers to other areas of your life. It's like training for resilience in thirty second intervals.

If you want to start building this habit, begin with just splashing water on your wrists when you feel tired. That's your entry point. Your brain will start associating this tiny action with feeling more alert, and before you know it, you'll be reaching for water instead of coffee.

Coming Back to Your Senses

Modern life has this sneaky way of pulling us into our heads and keeping us there. We spend entire days lost in abstract thinking, future worrying, or past replaying. The five senses scan is your express route back to the present moment, and it takes about thirty seconds.

Set a gentle reminder on your phone to go off once an hour. When it does, close your eyes and tune into each of your senses one by one. Start with taste. What do you notice in your mouth right now? Maybe it's the lingering flavour of your morning tea or just the neutral taste of saliva. Then smell. What scents are around you? Your colleague's perfume, the faint smell of lunch from the kitchen, the cleaning products someone used earlier.

Move to touch. Feel your clothes against your skin, the temperature of the air, the texture of whatever you're sitting on. Then sound. Notice the obvious noises first, then listen for the subtle background sounds you usually filter out. Finally, open your eyes and find one visual detail you hadn't consciously noticed before.

This practice rewires your attention patterns. Instead of strengthening those neural pathways that keep you stuck in mental loops, you're building new ones that connect you to immediate reality. People who do this regularly report feeling more emotionally stable and less anxious. Their nervous systems learn to anchor in what's actually happening instead of what might happen.

Digital Sunset

If you struggle with sleep, chances are your phone is part of the problem. The blue light tricks your brain into thinking it's still daytime, which completely messes with your natural sleep hormones. The digital sunset protocol helps you work with your body's natural rhythms instead of against them.

Set your phone to automatically switch to warm, dimmed display settings an hour before you want to sleep. Most phones can do this automatically now, so you don't have to remember. When those settings kick in, it's your cue for a brief wind down ritual.

Brain Dump on Paper

Your mind is probably running a constant background commentary of thoughts, worries, plans, and random observations. Stream of consciousness writing gives all that mental chatter somewhere to go besides round and round in your head.

Grab any piece of paper and write continuously for three to five minutes. The only rule is that you never stop writing. If you can't think of anything, write about not being able to think of anything. If emotions come up, write about the emotions. If you think what you're writing is rubbish, write about thinking it's rubbish.

Don't worry about grammar, spelling, or making sense. Let single words, incomplete sentences, emotional outbursts, or random observations fill the page. You can even doodle if that's what wants to come out.

This practice interrupts your mind's habit of cycling the same thoughts over and over. When you externalise these ideas, you signal to your brain that it doesn't need to keep holding onto them. Many people discover patterns in their thinking that they never noticed whilst everything was swirling around internally.

Breath as Your Superpower

Of all the tools available for managing stress and anxiety, breathing is probably the most underestimated. It's always available, completely free, and incredibly effective.

Set gentle reminders to go off every couple of hours during your day. When prompted, spend just one minute breathing intentionally using the box pattern. Breathe in slowly through your nose for four counts, hold for four, breathe out through your mouth for four, hold empty for four. Repeat until your minute is up.

You can do this anywhere. In traffic, waiting in queues, walking between meetings, even during stressful conversations.

Pay special attention to moments when you notice tension, anxiety, or irritation starting to build. These are perfect cues for breath work. Instead of letting stress escalate, you interrupt it early with conscious breathing. With practice, your breath becomes a reliable tool for navigating daily challenges with more calm and clarity.

Making It Stick

Several years into practising tiny habits, I went through a particularly challenging period. Old emotional pain that I thought I'd dealt with started surfacing unexpectedly.

My usual instinct was to stay busy, work harder, think my way out of the discomfort. But this time, I had these micro practices as a different option. During that difficult week, I gave myself extra time each day to journal, meditate, and breathe. Placing ice packs on my chest for short intervals helped calm my body's stress response. It sounds strange, but the cold seemed to ground me, pulling my attention back to the present and slowing my mind's frantic racing.

I also committed fully to ETF, tapping. I tapped on the fear that I'd never be good enough. I tapped on the worry that if I slowed down, everything would fall apart. I tapped on insecurities that had been with me since childhood, beliefs I'd inherited without ever consciously choosing them.

Some sessions brought dramatic releases with tears. Others were quiet. In the past, I would have abandoned these gentle approaches the moment things got emotionally intense. But that week taught me that healing happens through slow, steady unwinding of old tension, supported by small habits cultivated over time.

When the storm passed, these tools that once seemed too small to matter had proven their strength when I needed them most. My nervous system had developed a new baseline.

Challenges that used to send me spiralling now felt manageable. This is what neuroplasticity looks like in practice. Every time you repeat one of these micro habits, you're literally rewiring your brain. It's like going to the gym for your nervous system.

KEY TAKEAWAYS

1 | Late one day after putting my children to bed, I realised I hadn't felt present all day. I'd answered emails in the car park whilst waiting for their activities to finish and barely tasted dinner. My head was so crowded with "what ifs" that I couldn't settle. I lay in bed wide awake, pulse racing over absolutely nothing, as if I were running a marathon in place but not moving forward.

2 | When my coach asked if I'd ever tried "dropping into my body," I laughed. In my mind, feelings were unpredictable and logic thrived in my head. I'd spent years solving problems with my intellect, so slowing down to feel them felt naive. But thinking my way out wasn't working anymore. My head was simply a receiver picking up old programming that I'd never consciously updated.

3 | Small habits work because they sneak past our psychological alarm bells. When we try massive changes, our brains flood us with doubt and fear. But one push up uses the same habit forming mechanisms as fifty. The difference is psychological momentum. One feels doable, fifty feels like climbing Mount Everest. Every action is like casting a vote for who you want to be.

4 | The cold water wake up call beats that fourth cup of coffee. Walk to the nearest sink and splash cold water on your face and wrists for ten seconds, focusing on temples and pulse points. Take five slow breaths. Cold water jolts your nervous system awake differently than caffeine. It activates your vagus nerve, your body's natural reset button, giving immediate alertness without jitters or crashes.

5 | Digital sunset helps you work with natural sleep rhythms instead of against them. Set your phone to automatically switch to warm, dimmed settings an hour before sleep. Blue light tricks your brain into thinking it's daytime, completely messing with sleep hormones. When those settings kick in, it's your cue for wind down rituals.

6 | Brain dump on paper gives mental chatter somewhere to go besides round and round in your head. Write continuously for three to five minutes without stopping. If you can't think of anything, write about not thinking of anything. Don't worry about grammar or making sense. This interrupts your mind's habit of cycling the same thoughts repeatedly.

CHAPTER 9

DISCOVERING BALANCE

MY YEAR IN THE PARK

"Never get so busy making a living that you forget to make a life." — Dolly Parton, country music singer-songwriter, actress, businesswoman, and philanthropist

The late afternoon sun warmed my neck as vanilla ice cream melted between my fingers. My six year old son's infectious giggle rose above the clatter of school gates. His bright voice, clear as spring birdsong, rang out. "Dad'll take me!"

Whether a birthday party invitation, Saturday errands, or a quick dash to the store for glitter glue, the answer was always the same. My husband and I had built our family life as equal partners. Team Gardner, we called ourselves, sharing bath time, bedtime stories, and breakfast negotiations. Yet somehow, my son had begun defaulting to his father for everything that mattered.

The moment of reckoning arrived on a crisp spring afternoon. I stood beside our kitchen island, filing Tesco board papers into plastic sleeves, when my son bounded in, clutching a crumpled party invitation. "Dad'll take me," he announced once again before darting away.

The night before, I had missed another bedtime. The final budget read out had stretched past ten o'clock, forcing me to catch the last train from St. Pancras. I had tiptoed through our front door after midnight, convincing myself I was managing everything perfectly. But the scoreboard that mattered most told a different story. My son's attachment patterns revealed the truth I had been avoiding.

When had I become the backup parent? How many "just one more meeting" sessions had stolen story time? What would another year of this pace cost our family? At three in the morning, I padded to the bathroom and stared at my reflection in the harsh fluorescent light. Mascara rings circled my eyes. A stranger wearing my pyjamas stared back.

Morning broke clear and sharp. I showered, dried my hair, and slipped into the navy jacket that projected competence. Coffee in hand, I typed an email requesting ten minutes with my director. My palms grew clammy, but my resolve felt steady. When he ushered me into his glass office, I spoke before courage could evaporate. "I need a career break." He blinked twice. "How long?" he asked.

"A year," I replied, surprising myself with the certainty in my voice. The answer felt solid as granite. Sometimes the pendulum must swing dramatically to find its centre.

By September, I had exchanged my corporate lanyard for a school-run high-visibility vest. Every weekday at 2:55 PM, I waited outside my son's school clutching a 99 Flake. He would burst through the doors, face glowing with delight, and fling himself at me as though I had returned from a long sea voyage. We would wander to the park beside the preschool, debating the perfect ratio of chocolate sprinkles and inventing secret handshakes. We called that sabbatical "The Year of Ice Cream in the Park," though ice cream served merely as the entry ticket. What we purchased was time.

There were unhurried minutes to examine ladybirds, long afternoons exploring dinosaur facts, and quiet pockets where a mother could simply exist. By Christmas, my son no longer announced his parental preferences. He simply reached for my hand.

A decade later, whenever someone insists they cannot step away from their career, I share this story. Dramatic changes in life are occasionally the only sensible response. A short, decisive correction can prevent a long, slow capsize.

THE ANTI-CAREER LADDER

Most personal development thinking follows a ladder approach. You start at the bottom with basic needs like safety and shelter, then methodically climb upwards towards things like self actualisation and purpose. Maslow's famous hierarchy suggests you can't pursue higher goals until you've sorted your foundations. For anyone living in the real world, this feels both unrealistic and paralysing.

Life doesn't work like that. You don't tick off boxes in order before moving to the next level. You might be nursing a streaming cold whilst working on your novel or grieving your grandmother whilst paying the electricity bill. The ladder model suggests these pursuits are somehow wrong, that you should wait for perfect circumstances before chasing what matters to you.

Wellbeing research points to something different. Instead of climbing upwards through stages, thriving people maintain strength across multiple areas of life simultaneously. Think of it like a platter instead of a ladder. When one side of the plate empties, the others keep you feeling nourished.

In 2024, a large Gallup survey looked at 128,000 people across 160 countries and found something fascinating.

Strong friendships cut the wellbeing impact of short term unemployment by half. Good physical health helped people cope with financial stress. These cross connections between different life areas contradict everything the ladder model tells us. Psychologists call this the shock absorber effect. Just like your car's suspension stops every pothole from ruining your ride, strength in one area of life cushions blows in another. Someone with solid friendships handles job loss completely differently than someone who's socially isolated. Someone who's physically fit deals with money worries with more emotional resilience than someone whose health is already compromised.

The brilliant thing about understanding life as a platter is that it explains why perfect balance isn't the goal. You don't need every side to be equally strong at all times. Sometimes your career needs intense focus during a big project launch. Other periods call for pouring energy into relationships during family transitions or health crises. What matters is conscious choice about where to direct your attention. Adults naturally rebalance their priorities every seven to ten years according to researchers. Graduation, first house purchase, becoming a parent, menopause, children leaving home, retirement, and so on. Each major transition triggers a reshuffling of what matters most.

Recognising these natural cycles stops you from panicking when temporary imbalance feels permanent.

The platter approach honours how messy and complex human life actually is whilst still giving you a framework to work with. Unlike rigid systems that demand you be consistent all the time, it accommodates the natural rhythms of being human. It recognises that wellbeing comes from interconnected strength across your whole life. It's not climbing an imaginary ladder one rung at a time.

PLATTER VS LADDER

Through decades of research and coaching experience, I've distilled life balance into seven areas. Think of them as different sections on a dinner plate, each needing attention for you to feel well and resilient. Together, they give you a way to navigate all the competing demands of modern life.

1. Health covers your physical energy. This includes everything from your fitness level to how you recover, from understanding nutrition to being aware of what your body needs. When your health is shaky, everything else becomes harder and less sustainable.

2. Wellbeing is about your mental and emotional state, the way you talk to yourself, and how you handle stress. This internal world shapes how you see challenges, deal with setbacks, and stay steady during rough patches. It includes things like mindfulness, understanding your emotions, and building psychological strength.

3. Relationships are your family connections, friendships, community ties, and intimate partnerships. We're social beings, and the quality of our connections affects our physical health and mental stability. This area needs active care and consistent attention.

4. Vocation represents work that feels meaningful, whether you're paid for it or not. This goes beyond climbing the career ladder to include having a sense of purpose, making a contribution, and using your unique talents to serve something bigger than yourself. Meaningful work gives you energy rather than draining it.

5. Money is your financial wellbeing. Not just accumulating wealth, but using money as a tool for creating freedom, security, and positive impact. It includes how you earn, spend, save, and give.

6. Time and Freedom reflect your pace of your life. It includes being able to say no to things that don't fit, creating space for spontaneity, and designing life rhythms that support your energy.

7. Passion and Play cover hobbies, creative expression, intellectual curiosity, and exploration. These pursuits often feel frivolous but they're crucial for maintaining motivation, preventing burnout, and connecting you with joy and wonder. They expand who you are beyond your professional role whilst nurturing parts of your personality that goal focused activities can't reach.

Each of these focal points is a section on a plate. When one gets neglected, the whole plate feels unbalanced. You might pile too much onto work whilst barely touching relationships. Or load up on health activities whilst ignoring your creative side. The beauty of thinking about it as a plate is that you can see where you need to add more or perhaps where you've got too much going on.

Different seasons of life naturally emphasise different sections of the plate. New parents focus heavily on relationships and health. People whose children have left home might rediscover passion projects. The plate approach adapts to changing circumstances whilst helping you maintain strength across all areas.

GREEDY JOBS

Something fundamental has shifted in how work operates, and it's making balanced living nearly impossible for millions of people. Sociologists Youngjoo Cha and Kim Weeden studied four thousand dual income American families and discovered what they called "greedy jobs." These are positions that demand not just long hours, but complete availability. Think law firms, consulting companies, investment banks, and senior management roles where being "always on" is a required for advancement.

Jobs demanding more than fifty hours weekly plus constant availability eroded family satisfaction twice as fast as the extra income could compensate. What makes this particularly devastating is the timing. Just as women became the most educated generation in history, the jobs that require those degrees started rewarding extreme availability above all else.

Four decades ago, people working more than fifty hours a week earned fifteen percent less per hour than those working standard full time schedules. By 2000, this penalty had become a premium. Today, people working fifty hours or more earn up to eight percent more per hour than similar people working thirty five to forty nine hours. The reward for being available around the clock has skyrocketed.

Harvard economist Claudia Goldin puts it bluntly. "It's this system we put in place in the era of 'Mad Men' and we're stuck with, and we're sort of hammering away at in small ways rather than taking the whole thing down."

This creates an impossible choice for families. To maximise household income whilst still managing children and home life, it becomes logical for one parent to take the intensive job whilst the other takes something more manageable. In most couples, that usually means the woman steps back. Not because she's less ambitious, but because the math of modern work makes any other arrangement financially devastating.

A lawyer featured in New York Times research on this phenomenon explains the harsh reality. "I think I'd be happier in life if I was home more with my children and if I didn't have the same stress at work," he said, "but I think this was the best decision for our family." He works sixty to eighty hour weeks.

Lewis Coser coined the term "greedy institutions" in 1974 to describe organisations that "seek exclusive and undivided loyalty." Originally applied to things like the military or religious orders, this concept now describes mainstream professional careers. Technology has made the problem worse. Workers are more easily reachable and expected to be responsive across time zones.

Business has become more global, meaning someone is always awake somewhere expecting responses. The rise of winner take all economics means the gap between high and low earners has widened dramatically, making the stakes feel higher.

The human cost is that 20% percent of fathers now work at least fifty hours a week, whereas 6% of mothers do. What's particularly sad is how this reproduces inequality whilst appearing meritocratic. The people who can work greedy jobs are those with support systems at home. This usually means having a partner who can handle sick children and elderly parents. Single parents, regardless of talent or education, are automatically excluded from these opportunities.

This level of intensity is unsustainable and ultimately counterproductive. Instead, we need to restructure how work gets done. Companies that have experimented with more predictable schedules and genuine flexibility have found they can maintain high performance without requiring employees to sacrifice their humanity.

APPLYING THE PLATE MODEL

By 2024, I'd left the fluorescent lit world behind and started the Ohana Foundation, global movement to empower people to feel safe loving themselves. Client emails kept flooding in, which felt great as a new founder, but I could sense that familiar unsteady feeling creeping back.

This time, instead of needing another year off to reset everything, I tried something different. Tiny daily adjustments that, when they add up over time, keep everything balanced.

Getting Health Right First

Monday and Friday mornings at seven became untouchable time with Liz, my personal trainer. She's an ex Royal Marine who won't accept any excuses, and frankly, that's exactly what I needed. Those two sessions each week became the foundation that everything else was built on.

Back in my corporate days, I'd go to the gym then reward myself with enormous pastries, which rather defeated the point. This time, I let the endorphins be the reward. Those natural highs replaced the adrenaline rush of constant crisis management, giving me energy that actually lasted.

Walking ten thousand steps daily with Fergus, our cockapoo, turned exercise from something I had to do into something we did together. If I tried to skip our woodland walk, he'd park himself by the front door with those accusatory brown eyes until I gave in. Those walks became my thinking time. Being outside and moving naturally reset my nervous system better than any meeting ever could.

What surprised me was how everything connected. Better exercise meant better sleep. Better sleep meant better food choices. Better food choices gave me more energy for everything else. Health stopped being something I fitted around work and became what made work possible in the first place.

Daily Maintenance

I squeezed a five minute mental check in between switching the kettle on and pouring my coffee, when the day still felt manageable. Three proper belly breaths, then one honest line in my journal asking what needed gentle attention today. Sometimes the answer was "call Mum." Other days it was "take a nap this afternoon."

Getting clear on what I needed early stopped the emotional pile up that used to explode into weekend meltdowns. This tiny practice worked better than all those elaborate meditation routines that needed perfect conditions.

The daily check in helped me recognise my emotional patterns and catch stress before it turned into a crisis. Some days I felt anxious about the business. Other days, parenting teenagers felt overwhelming. Instead of shoving these feelings down, I learned to acknowledge them and ask what they were trying to tell me.

Letting Relationships Be

My husband thinks in practical, concrete terms whilst my mind wanders. I used to drag him to every workshop and retreat, convinced he needed enlightening. Now I appreciate that he keeps me grounded when I float off into the clouds. Dropping my improvement project for him made our marriage much softer. With the kids, I stopped being the homework police and started being more curious about how they were actually doing. Fewer interrogations about whether they'd finished their assignments and more questions about what was going on in their hearts. Teenagers rarely give you straight answers, but they notice when you care enough to ask.

The big shift was letting go of control. I worked on creating the kind of atmosphere where people felt safe to be honest. This worked much better than my previous approach of rules and expectations. Relationships got better when I stopped trying to fix the people in them.

Work Success Looks Different Now

Corporate life measured everything in massive budgets and quarterly growth targets that had to keep getting bigger. Now I measure impact by the light in people's eyes. If my workshop has two participants instead of eight, that's still two lives touched. This shift in thinking, inspired by watching a ZZ Top documentary where they played their first ever gig to just one person and gave it everything they had, freed me from the numbers obsession.

I had to retrain my internal scorekeeper. Meaningful work needs different ways of measuring success based on purpose. Part of redefining success meant letting go of specific outcomes whilst staying committed to doing excellent work. I could control my preparation, quality, and presence. Results depended on things like timing, market conditions, and whether people were ready for what I offered.

Money as Flow

Mum used to say I burned through money faster than Irn Bru loses its fizz. I carried that story for decades, approaching finances with anxiety and scarcity thinking that made the problem worse. Seeing money as neutral energy flowing through my life completely changed how I dealt with abundance and planning.

Every spending decision reflects my values now. Investing in health, relationships, or meaningful work feels natural. Generosity comes easily. This stopped the shame spirals that used to sabotage my financial planning.

Every time I hear the word "love," I picture a ten pound note flying towards me. This rewired my subconscious associations with money from fear to flow. Money became a tool for creating freedom instead of a constant source of worry.

Mastering the Art of Saying No

In my people pleasing days, I'd spend months recovering emotionally from turning down one request. I once declined something that didn't fit my priorities and spent eighteen months questioning whether I'd made the right choice. Now, using some EFT and tapping, I bounce back within a week. Each successful "no" made the next one easier and less emotionally draining. I created a clear hierarchy with family at the top, meaningful work second, and everything else negotiable based on my current capacity and energy.

Having prepared language ready eliminated the pressure of making decisions on the spot. Saying something like "I don't have the capacity to give this the attention it deserves right now" shows respect for both the request and my own limitations.

Regular Creative Experiments

Little Wendy loved art class, but adult Wendy forgot creativity existed. I made a quarterly deal with myself to try one playful activity for at least four sessions before deciding whether to continue. Pottery, life drawing, wild swimming, and singing became experiments in rediscovering different parts of myself.

The four session minimum stopped me from giving up too quickly. Most adults avoid new activities because of performance pressure, but getting good at things was never the point. Connecting with different aspects of my personality was what mattered. This brought back curious, experimental qualities that corporate life had squashed.

Some activities clicked and continued. Others didn't fit and ended without guilt. The experimenting itself was valuable, preventing my identity from getting stuck in narrow definitions of what I was capable of or interested in.

BALANCING TOOLS

Making the plate model work in daily life needs specific tools that turn all this research into something you can actually use. These methods give you frameworks for keeping everything steady whilst adapting to whatever life throws at you, without needing to completely overhaul how you live.

Work in Natural Rhythms

Set a timer for ninety minutes during mentally demanding work, then step away for at least ten minutes regardless of how well things are going or what deadlines are looming. During these breaks, do something that uses different parts of your brain like gentle stretching, making tea, or just looking out the window at something far away. This matches your body's natural performance cycles.

Many high achievers hate this idea. But research shows that forcing yourself to continue beyond your natural energy cycles actually produces worse results. The framework keeps you performing well across longer periods instead of achieving brief peaks followed by crashes.

Joy Anchors

Pick one thing each week that brings you pleasure and protect it fiercely, no matter what else comes up. Friday evening pizza with the family, Sunday morning swims, Tuesday book club. Guard this commitment as seriously as you would an important business meeting.

These joy anchors work as guaranteed pleasure points in uncertain weeks. Knowing that Friday evening belongs to family time or Sunday morning is yours alone lets you be more flexible during other periods. These rituals become emotional reset buttons that stop stress from building up.

Recovery Menu

Give yourself variety in how you restore energy by developing lists of options including two minute breathing exercises, twenty second stretches, five minute garden walks, or brief meditation sessions. Post these somewhere visible and experiment with different approaches throughout your day.

What feels restorative changes based on your current stress levels, energy state, and environment. Having multiple recovery options ensures you can find appropriate restoration regardless of how much time you have.

Time = Money

Transform abstract balance concepts into concrete weekly planning by calculating your upcoming week's waking hours, typically around one hundred and twelve total. Allocate time blocks to each life.

This reveals gaps between what you say matters and where your time actually goes. Many people discover they unconsciously spend time on low value activities. Regular reviews create awareness and enable course corrections before drift becomes a major imbalance.

The plate approach works because it's flexible. You maintain strength across different life areas whilst allowing for natural ups and downs. The goal is to make conscious choices about where to spend your time and energy based on what actually matters to you.

KEY TAKEAWAYS

1 | My six year old son's response to everything became "Dad'll take me!" Whether birthday parties or Saturday errands, he always chose his father. I'd convinced myself I was managing everything perfectly, but my son's attachment patterns revealed I had become the backup parent.

2 | I walked into my director's glass office. "I need a career break." When he asked how long, I surprised myself with the certainty in my voice. "A year." By September, I'd exchanged my corporate lanyard for a school run high visibility vest. We called it "The Year of Ice Cream in the Park," though ice cream was just the entry ticket. What we purchased was time.

3 | Most personal development follows a ladder approach where you tick off boxes before moving to the next level. Life doesn't work like that. Wellbeing research points to something different. Think of it like a platter instead of a ladder.

4 | Sociologists studied four thousand dual income families and discovered "greedy jobs." Jobs demanding more than fifty hours a week eroded family satisfaction twice as fast as the extra income could compensate.

5 | A 2024 Gallup survey of 128,000 people across 160 countries found that strong friendships cut the wellbeing impact of short term unemployment by half. Good physical health helped people cope with financial stress. This is called the shock absorber effect. Just like your car's suspension stops every pothole from ruining your ride, strength in one area cushions blows in another.

6 | I created seven life areas that need attention for resilience. Health covers physical energy, sleep, nutrition, and movement. Wellbeing includes mental state and stress management. Relationships cover family, friends, and community. Vocation represents meaningful work. Money involves financial wellbeing as a tool for freedom. Time and Freedom reflect life's pace and your ability to say no. Passion and Play cover hobbies and creative expression.

7 | Monday and Friday mornings at seven became untouchable time with Liz, my ex Royal Marine personal trainer who won't accept excuses. Those sessions became the foundation everything else was built on. Walking ten thousand steps daily with Fergus, our cockapoo, turned exercise from something I had to do into something we did together. Health stopped being something I fitted around work and became what made work possible.

CHAPTER 10

BELIEF ARCHITECTURE

SHIFTING BELIEFS

"I am no longer accepting the things I cannot change. I am changing the things I cannot accept." — Angela Y. Davis

Mum used to introduce me to strangers with a joke polished by repetition. I'd "come out the womb with champagne tastes on an Irn-Bru budget." The punchline landed with a laugh. The subtext landed like a warning. Watch yourself, hen, or you'll end up skint.

By twelve, I was a one-girl shift rota. Early mornings at the ice-cream van, Saturdays at Wimpy, babysitting past midnight. By Monday, the wages had evaporated into cinema tickets for friends I needed to like me, and bargain-bin Levi's I convinced myself would change who I was. Back home, the debit-card slip might as well have been a confession. "Hole in your pocket big enough to drive the Flying Scotsman through," Mum would mutter.

Dad played by different rules entirely. He had an impulse. Fish and chips, "because why not," holidays booked on a whim, and a new telly. Their marriage balanced like a seesaw. Mum counted Green Shield stamps. Dad purchased a karaoke machine we used three times.

Two philosophies took root in one girl. Scarcity whispered from one shoulder, rebellion from the other, and I learned to call the argument personality. In my twenties I earned more than any Rodgers before me, yet by Friday I was buying shoes that blistered my feet and my conscience. On Mondays I'd open Excel and flagellate myself with formulas.

Then came lockdown. Shops shuttered. Parcels from ME+EM stopped arriving with their fizzy hit of possibility. Without the spend-guilt carousel squeaking in the background, the silence was deafening. One evening in April, in a tiny square on a Zoom screen, a meditation teacher offered six words that finally cut through the fog: "A belief is simply a thought you practise."

Mum's "you'll end up with nothing" and Dad's "stuff it, splurge" had been ventriloquising my adult choices for decades. Loyal, loud... and outdated. That night I realised how good I'd become at following their scripts. But scripts can be rewritten.

Your brain is a prediction engine learning a three-part dance.

Default Mode Network: daydreaming, time-travel, replaying arguments you didn't win. It supplies the backdrop for "who I am" stories.

Salience Network: acts like a bouncer, flagging what matters, ie. danger, novelty, opportunity, and what can be ignored.

Fronto-Parietal Control Network: the choreographer, helping you plan, focus, and redirect attention when it wanders.

When they keep time, new information threads its way without much drama. When they fall out of step, familiar stories drown out contradictory facts. A repeated thought, like money is scarce, or I'm terrible with numbers, etches a groove. According to neuroscientists, neurons that fire together wire together. Beliefs also game the evidence. The brain, efficient to a fault, loves to be right. Present it with mixed feedback and it will highlight whatever confirms the script and dim anything that contradicts it. You pay the electricity bill on time for eight months and forget it by dinner. Overdraw your account once, remember it for a decade. The mind keeps receipts.

Expectation shapes outcomes too. In one classic school study, teachers were quietly told a random subset of pupils was poised to "bloom." Those children's scores rose more than their peers' thanks to being on the receiving end of a warmer tone and slightly more challenging questions. Micro-behaviours, repeated, become identity.

Under extreme stress, expectations leave fingerprints on our biology. Studies of famine and catastrophe suggest that intense scarcity may alter the brain chemicals on stress-response genes, and, intriguingly, related patterns show up in their adult children.

In families, one child is "the spender," another "the careful one," a third "the worrier." Ten years later, the labels map eerily onto bank statements and career choices. We're unique, yes. We're also exquisitely imitative.

HOPE AND HELPLESSNESS

When the young psychologist Martin Seligman studied why dogs, and later people, stopped trying, he described a phenomenon we now recognise as learned helplessness. But Seligman also noticed something else. Change the story, and you change the outcome. He called the alternative learned optimism.

His practical tool compresses a lifetime of therapy into five letters. Think of it as **ABC → DE**:

- **A**ctivating event: you're invited for an interview.
- **B**elief: I won't get this job, I'm hopeless.
- **C**onsequence: you lack confidence, you don't get the job

Most of us stop here and declare the emotion "truth." Two more steps change the game:

- **D**ispute: Is this belief accurate?
- **E**nergise: You prepare, arrive more confident, and get it.

Run **ABCDE** on paper for five minutes a day for two weeks and you'll begin to hear the difference between your mother's caution, your father's rebellion, and your own present reality.

If you like a wider lens, Seligman later gathered the ingredients of wellbeing into **PERMA**.

Positive emotion
Engagement
Relationships
Meaning
Achievement.

Think of them as five dials you can tune while you re-author your money story. We've been nudging those dials throughout this book.

THE EDITABLE BRAIN

For years scientists thought adult brains were final drafts. Then came decades of evidence to the contrary. Learn a language, practise the piano, meditate most days for eight weeks. Scan the brain before and after and you'll see change.

Connections strengthen between the prefrontal regions that help you choose wisely and the deeper emotion centres that shout "threat!" too often. Practice, especially deliberate practice, teaches the prediction engine to expect something better. Beliefs upgrade through repetition. The old groove, ie. I'll never have enough, fades through disuse. I can build enoughness deepens. Like fitness, plasticity is available at every age. Like fitness, it's earned in small, consistent sessions.

Insight is lovely. It's also slippery. To make "a belief is a thought you practise" real, I needed steps I could do any night of the week, even when I was tired. Here's the toolkit I used.

1) Belief Cartography

Take one stubborn thought. Write it exactly as your inner critic speaks it. Now map four columns:

1. Exact words: “I’m useless with money” is not the same as “I sometimes panic when I look at my balance.”

2. Emotional load: Name the feeling, rate intensity (0–10), and note where it lands in your body.

3. Evidence for: Memories, cultural messages, family sayings. Collect them. (You’ve been doing this unconsciously for years.)

4. Evidence against: Hunt the counter-examples you usually ignore, such as months you paid everything on time, or choices you handled well.

Don’t use column four to shame column three and don’t wait for certainty before moving on.

2) Back-Testing

Treat beliefs like hypotheses. Choose one ("I'm terrible with money"), set a period (last 12 months), define metrics (on-time payments, savings rate, debt balance), and pull the data.

Where the numbers disconfirm the story, underline them. Where they confirm it, ask, "What single tweak would improve this metric by 1% next month?"

3) Future-Self Rehearsal

Write a dated letter from your future self five years from today. Past tense. I checked my accounts each evening without dread. I kept a small "future you fund" for curious pleasures. When an unexpected expense arrived, I took one slow breath and consulted my plan.

4) Visual Primers

Create a small collage that feels like "enoughness." It may include open hands, green shoots, or a well-worn footpath. Add two or three words that work for you, such as "flow," "steward," and "room." Tape it somewhere you pass often.

5) Daily Micro-Reps

Tiny behaviours that don't harm the nervous system:

• The Money Minute: each evening, open your accounts. Note one choice you're pleased with. Close the app.

• Language Lag: add "yet" or "so far" to any absolute that escapes ("I can't budget... yet"). It sounds tiny. It works.

• Stop-Signal: when you hear the family phrase "we can't afford that," replace it with "we're not choosing that right now because we're choosing this."

THE WORDS THAT RAISED US

If beliefs are practised thoughts, what did we practise first? Usually, inherited lines:

- "We're not that sort of people."
- "Don't get too big for your boots."
- "Money doesn't grow on trees."
- "Be grateful for what you're given."

At the time, each had a job. Some may have kept us safe, others may have kept us out of debt. The trouble starts when the sentence outruns the season. "Be grateful" becomes "never ask." "We're not that sort of people" becomes "we don't try." A practical way to loosen inherited lines:

1. Collect them. Walk round your home with a notebook. What sayings surface at the front door, with the bills, and around the biscuit tin?

2. Translate them. What were these phrases protecting us from? Embarrassment, risk, overspending?

3. Write the modern version. From "We can't afford it" to "If we want it, we'll find a way that doesn't harm Future Us."

For years I thought my spend-guilt-repeat cycle was a willpower lesson. It turned out to be about identity. Underneath the purchases were quieter beliefs:

- I spend to belong.
- Frugality means shameful lack.
- Others deserve my money more than I do.

Once I named them, I could honour the parts of me that learned those feelings. "Of course you wanted to belong." This empowered me to practise something new.

A template for uncovering beliefs beneath sticky behaviours:

- Cue (what precedes it?) → I see a sale. I feel lonely.
- Behaviour → I tap "buy now."
- Immediate payoff → Hit of dopamine.
- Hidden belief → Belonging is purchasable.

Then ask What's a truer belief I'd rather practise? and What's one tiny behaviour that would prove it today?

- Truer belief: Belonging is earned through presence. Tiny proof: Text one friend to plan a walk.

- Truer belief: Comfort can be made. Tiny proof: Cook a simple, warm meal.

OUR BELIEFS

Beliefs About Money

The Two-Pot Rule - Any money that arrives is split immediately into "Future Me" and "Today Me." Even if it's £10, split it. This interrupts the belief that saving is punishment and replaces it with saving is part of life.

The Seven-Day Waitlist - Anything over a chosen threshold goes on a list for seven days. In that pause, picture where it will live and its first three uses, then check with "Future Me": does this fit the person in your five-year letter? After seven days, if you still want it, buy it and enjoy it.

The Generosity Line Item - Make giving small and non-negotiable. (If big is easy and small is hard, you've found a belief worth exploring.) Give £2 a week to a school breakfast club or a neighbour's fundraiser. The belief practised here is that I am resourceful and kind.

Beliefs at Home

I used to think my job as a parent was to fix things. Mostly, by accident, I was fixing beliefs. Children learn who they are from how we meet their ordinary mess.

Three adjustments changed our household atmosphere:

1. From "What were you thinking?" to "What did you need?"
2. From "We can't afford that" to "How can we plan for it?"
3. From "Be careful" to "I trust your judgment."

When old scripts reappear, name them quickly. The evening my daughter asked for hot Ribena while upset, I heard my mother's voice saying, "Stop being so needy." Instead, I took one breath, put the kettle on, and said, "Thanks for telling me what would help."

My children began creating their own interrupts. "Mum, you're doing that money stress thing."

Beliefs at Work

Groups also believe, and then become their beliefs. Teams that treat money as fuel for status burn people out to keep the engine roaring. Organisations whisper identity to their people in ten thousand small ways. If you have even a sliver of influence in your organisation, you have an opportunity to shift your company's narrative:

- Replace "urgent" with "important by" in emails.
- When a forecast is missed, ask, "What did we learn?"
- Celebrate "kept promises" as loudly as "won deals."

Beliefs We Inherit

History itself can become a whisper in the blood. Maybe there was a layoff that hollowed a father's savings or a winter the ration card ran out. Children devour the emotions adults don't acknowledge and mistake them for the weather of the world.

If you suspect you're carrying something from before your time, try this gentle practice:

1. Name the era → "The year my father lost his job," "the winter Nana rationed bread," "the move that broke my mother's heart."

2. Name the inheritance → "Never trust employers," "everything good disappears," "pick up and don't get attached."

3. Offer thanks → At one point, that belief kept someone alive.

4. Offer an addendum → "And in my era, it's safe to save." "And in my era, stability can be built."

Write the old belief on a scrap of paper and the new belief beside it. Fold them together and plant them under a seedling. Watch what grows.

A CLOSING THREAD

This story began on a cold platform at Euston. A girl from Glasgow with a cheap suitcase, a loud heart, and a ticket pointing south.

It moves through offices lit long past midnight, past a delivery room that fell silent, past a crash on the motorway, a school gate at 2:55, and a boardroom where someone finally admits they're not all right. If you lay the scenes end to end, they look less like a ladder and more like a path someone made with their own feet.

For years I tried to outrun my own sense of self. I worked as if speed could keep sorrow from catching up. Colleagues called me "the machine" and I wore the name like armour. When Hannah was born sleeping, I simply kept going. The body objected in its own language... fevers, chest infections, and a tremor in the hands. Grief waited me out.

The first crack of light arrived quietly. "Actually, I'm not okay." I said it once. Suddenly, the scaffolding I'd built began to fall apart. Help appeared where I'd assumed there would be judgement. Therapy. A kinder commute. A husband spooning pasta into bowls. You think change will look like trumpets. It often sounds like an honest whisper.

Work shifted too. I spent years in rooms where I tried to be faintly less myself. Then I found a place where bright trainers and bright ideas were celebrated. People said "bring all of you" and meant it. I stopped speaking in jargon. Laughter returned, and results followed.

There were domestic revolutions. My son sprinting home, shouting "Dad'll take me!" again and again. I asked for a year and was startled to receive it. We named it the Year of Ice Cream in the Park. The budget spreadsheets vanished from the kitchen island and songbirds took their place. Some evenings he reached for my hand without checking whose turn it was. I had been waiting for permission. It turned out I only needed to apply for my own life.

Money had its say as well. Mum's thrift and Dad's "why not?" had been spinning inside my head for decades. During lockdown, a teacher offered six words that changed the room. "A belief is simply a thought you practise." I started splitting every pound into Today Me and Future Me. It was not revolutionary, just a small ritual, so dull and steady, that it rewired me when I wasn't looking.

Much of this book has been a search for ideas that build us up. The ones we inherit, "Don't get too big for your boots," or "We can't afford it," had jobs once. Some still do.

Others outlive their usefulness. I wrote new versions and taped them where I'd trip over them. "Mistakes are information." "There's always a way forward." "We're choosing this."

If you asked for the method, it's simple. Five minutes with a pen. One minute of breath. Cold water. The Money Minute. Naming the feeling rather than negotiating with it. Texting one friend to plan a walk. Moving £5 to Future Me.

Life will not always feel like it's on easy mode. Someone's summer vacation will still scroll past when your bank account blinks red. Old voices still clear their throats at inconvenient moments.

The difference is that you will recognise them, you will say their names, and you will take one small, boring action in favour of the person you're practising to be. That is the work. That is the hope.

If you have read this far, you now have the blueprint to live a more intentional and fulfilling life. You know how easily success can cost a self. You've felt what happens when rest returns, boundaries hold, and when generosity travels both directions across a kitchen table.

So, here is a quiet blessing for closing the covers.

Begin where you are. Name the season. Keep one promise so small it's almost silly. Write the sentence you need and put it where your hands will find it. Practise it out loud until the path underfoot feels different. Ask for help before you collapse. Offer it before you're asked. Let the people you love see you choose yourself, so they learn how to choose themselves too.

The girl on the platform didn't know any of this. She didn't know that machines can't love but humans can. If I could press one line into her palm, it would be the one that steadied me when everything else wobbled: we can only be what we can see.

You're welcome to borrow it.

ABOUT THE AUTHOR

Wendy Gardner is an author, speaker, and founder of The Ohana Foundation, where she helps "stuck" adults and girls reclaim their lives. A former "corporate machine" turned advocate for human sustainability, Wendy specialises in measurable well-being. When she isn't writing, she works directly with her "flock" through specialised workshops, coaching programmes, and keynote speaking.

www.ingramcontent.com/pod-product-compliance
Lightning Source LLC
LaVergne TN
LVHW010319220926
848484LV00004BB/804
9798218881610